BASIC BOOKS IN EDUCATION

Editor: *Kathleen O'Connor, B.Sc., Senior Lecturer in Education, Rolle College, Exmouth*
Advisory Editor: *D. J. O'Connor, M.A., Ph.D., Professor of Philosophy, University of Exeter*

Conduct:

An Introduction to Moral Philosophy

The author aims both to give a realistic and intelligible account of the scope and content of the subject and to provide a foundation upon which anyone who wishes to take his studies further can build. He begins by asking certain questions that arise within morality – about conflicting duties, egoism and altruism, guilt and responsibility – and goes on to consider more theoretical, philosophical questions about the logical status of moral judgements. Most of the main types of contemporary ethical theory are critically surveyed. A final chapter applies the findings of the earlier ones to questions concerning the relations between morality and science and religion.

Key words in the text are in SMALL CAPITALS, there are summaries and 'further reading' lists at the end of each chapter and there is a full bibliography, glossary and index.

By the same author

SEXUAL MORALITY (Hutchinson 1965)

Conduct:

An Introduction
to Moral Philosophy

R. F. ATKINSON, B.A., B.Phil.

PROFESSOR OF PHILOSOPHY
UNIVERSITY OF YORK

MACMILLAN
London . Melbourne . Toronto
1969

Published by
MACMILLAN AND CO LTD
Little Essex Street London WC2
and also at Bombay Calcutta and Madras
Macmillan South Africa (Publishers) Pty Ltd Johannesburg
The Macmillan Company of Australia Pty Ltd Melbourne
The Macmillan Company of Canada Ltd Toronto
Gill and Macmillan Ltd Dublin

Printed in Great Britain by
RICHARD CLAY (THE CHAUCER PRESS) LTD
Bungay, Suffolk

0-333-10240-4

010 8610

78502

170
202
ATK

Contents

Acknowledgements

I am greatly indebted to the following people who read the book in typescript and made many valuable suggestions: Mr D. J. Perrin, Mrs J. F. Stowers, Professor D. J. O'Connor. They have saved me from a number of errors and infelicities, but, are not, of course, to be held responsible for any which remain.

My grateful thanks are due also to Mrs M. Allinson who typed the manuscript with characteristic accuracy.

1 Introduction

MORAL PHILOSOPHY

MORAL PHILOSOPHY is, as one would expect, the philosophical study of morality, but it is perhaps less clear what makes a study philosophical, and conceptions of philosophy have varied greatly over the centuries.

'Philosophy' used to be closer in meaning to 'science' and was applied indifferently to what we now distinguish as natural and social science on the one hand, and philosophy proper on the other. The older usage survives in the phrase 'natural philosophy', meaning *physics*, which is still to be found in the calendars of some universities. In the eighteenth century it was quite common to think in terms of a distinction between natural and moral philosophy (or science). David Hume, for instance, had the ambition to be the Newton of the moral sciences. But even in this connection 'moral philosophy (science)' has a wider application than it has today. In addition to what is now thought of as moral philosophy, it covers such human or social sciences as psychology, sociology and economics, and indeed the propounding of first-order moral principles too.

At the very least a *threefold* distinction is needed. First, there are psychology, sociology, economics, etc. (once called the moral sciences) which, like physics, chemistry, etc. (the natural sciences) aim to ascertain facts and to explain them by bringing them under laws and theories. Then there is expressing views about what is good or bad, right or wrong, what ought or ought not to be done. For this there seems not to be a better word than 'MORALISING', though it has to be used without its usual disparaging overtone. The scientist deals in facts, the moralist in values. The one is concerned with what *is*, the other with what *ought to be*. But the philosopher is different again. His concern is CONCEPTS. He does not ask what things are good, what actions right (these are moralists' questions), but what does 'good' mean, what would count as a reason for deeming something good. Nor does he ask such psychological (factual or scientific) questions as at what age do children become capable of experiencing moral obligation, but enquires rather what is involved in the concept of obligation and under what circumstances would someone be held to be under obligation. Moralising is sometimes termed a *first-order* activity with a view to distinguishing it from moral philosophy, which is not moralising but the *second-order* study of it. Similarly, philosophy of science is the second-order study of first-order scientific thinking and procedure.

It does not, however, require a very careful examination of many of the classics of moral philosophy – writings of Plato and Aristotle, Butler, Hume, Kant, Mill, etc. – in order to see that they often contain a good deal that is not by contemporary standards strictly philosophical. This mainly reflects the way that the scope of philosophy has narrowed over the years. Economics, psychology, sociology, once the preserve of philosophers, have hived off and aspire to intellectual autonomy. Their practitioners are no longer pleased to be called philosophers. Moralising too, even of the most reflective kind, is now distinguished from philosophy as part of its subject matter. Inevitably, the question has arisen whether in the end anything will be left for philosophy *as such*, and naturally enough attempted answers stress what is distinctive about philosophy, what differentiates it from everything else. Recent moral philosophers have, on the whole, been much more self conscious than their predecessors about the nature of their subject, and their apparent narrowness of interest, their theoretical rather than practical bent, derives from this. It is important, particularly in an introduction to any part of philosophy, to convey a clear sense of what is and what is not philosophy. Though, of course, it does not follow that because something is not strictly philosophy it is uninteresting or unimportant in itself.

Conceptual enquiry, philosophy, may be and often is pursued for its own sake, without regard to its social or other utility, such as it is. The same is true of moral philosophy, in which, though its subject matter is the assessment of conduct, it is possible to take a purely theoretical interest. For someone concerned with the 'logic of adjectives', 'good' might be of interest only because its 'behaviour' differs somewhat from that of words like 'red', 'tall' and 'porous'. In the same sort of way, atheistical philosophers may be fascinated by the peculiarities of the concepts of omnipotence and creativity, and philistines concern themselves with the beautiful or with artistic truth. Strong first-order moral conviction or perplexity, is not a *necessary* qualification for taking up with moral philosophy, nor, alas, a *sufficient condition* for making a contribution to it. All the same, it is evident that many important moral philosophers have been driven to the subject by their strong practical concerns. They seek to clarify concepts because they see confusion as an obstacle to developing sensible views about how people should live and act. This sort of concern is conspicuous in Plato's Socrates, in Kant and, among contemporary writers, in Hare. The moral philosopher does not have to be a moralist, but the moralist cannot afford altogether to ignore the clarifications of philosophy.

Moral philosophy is not science, not even the scientific or historical study of the development of moral ideas in societies and individuals. But, on the one hand, the moral philosopher cannot reasonably be indifferent to the question whether the concepts he considers are those actually current, nor, on the other, is it possible to assess the implications of scientific or historical studies without some philosophical understanding of key moral concepts. The writings of Piaget, for instance, strongly suggest that a certain attitude to moral rules is immature; and Freudian theory seems to cast doubt on the authority of conscience. But, leaving aside questions of the *correctness* of the observations and soundness of the theories of Freud and Piaget, we still cannot determine what follows from them with regard to morality until we are clear about the concepts of conscience and moral rules.

Moral philosophy, as conceived in this book, is continuous with the rest of philosophy. It is philosophy focused on a particular subject-matter, morality. With this subject-matter nobody who has come through the first few years of life can possibly be unacquainted. The point of the next section is not to try to tell the reader what he must already know, but only to indicate the way in which the rather formal categories, and sometimes archaic terminology, of moral philosophy relate to the familiar phenomena of the moral life.[1]*

MORALITY

Moral philosophy is about morality. Frequently, to say the least, moral philosophers disagree. Sometimes this will be because they are making incompatible statements about the same thing, other-times perhaps they will be making possibly compatible statements about different things and their disagreement will be only apparent. The subject-matter of moral philosophy is not static. Uniformities there are, but there are also differences among the moralities of different times and places, of different societies.

A MORALITY is a set of beliefs current in a society about character and conduct, about what people should try to be or try to do. (The question whether there are several, equally 'valid', moralities, or one 'true' morality with various approximations to and deviations from it will be put aside for the moment.) Not all beliefs relating to character and conduct are, however, moral. Morality needs to be distinguished at least from law, custom, etiquette and politics, though it has to be recognised that these distinctions are not everywhere and everywhen as sharp as they are here and now. We, for instance, have specialised legislative and law enforcement institutions and it is, consequently, very easy to distinguish law and morality. A rule enacted by Parliament and enforced by the courts is unarguably the law, but Parliament and the courts *logically* cannot make a moral rule (i.e. we would not count a rule thus made as moral), though they could give a rule previously accepted as moral the force of law. In simple societies, without legislatures, courts, policemen, the distinction between law and morality is more elusive. Again, we are very conscious of the possibility of conflicts of interest between individuals and society. This reflects the nature of contemporary mass societies and their difference from, say, the city states of

* Small numbers refer to notes at the end of the chapter.

ancient Greece. Correspondingly, we may see the distinction between morals and politics in terms of the difference between autonomous, individual conviction and collective expediency. If I think something right, the dissent of fifty million fellow citizens does not prove me wrong. At most it should give me pause, but majority votes are not conclusive in morality. In politics, however, they count a great deal, for the politically right has to be found within the limits of the courses of action people generally will agree, or can be got, to go along with. In politics, unlike morals, 'good ideas' which nobody accepts, and which cannot therefore be implemented, are simply non-starters. As for the differences between morality, and custom and etiquette, differences which are widely recognised but not very easy to formulate, something seems to depend on the importance for human welfare of the sorts of character or conduct in question. Possibly connected with this is the feeling that customs and rules of etiquette are arbitrary and changeable in a way that the requirements of morality are not – I am, of course, at present attempting only a rough, preliminary, characterisation of the differences between moral and other views about character and conduct. Many of the issues that will be considered later on in the book would have to be decided before a really adequate account could be given.

Moral beliefs, then, are a certain sort of belief about people and their actions. Moral philosophers have presented such beliefs in different ways. Plato, for instance, discusses the meaning of abstract terms like 'virtue' or 'justice', typically understanding them very widely, so that 'justice' stands, not so much for one species of moral excellence, as for the whole of it. Something of ancient Greek moral attitudes comes across in Plato, although sober description was not his main concern. It does, however, seem to have been an important part of what Aristotle was trying to do. He offers a list of *virtues* – justice (in a sense narrower than Plato's), temperance, courage, magnaminity, prudence, and so on (the English words are not all of them adequate renderings of the Greek). Virtues are qualities of mind or character, dispositions revealed in choice and action, which are held to be morally admirable. Vices, of course, are morally *un*admirable characteristics.

This pattern of moral description was standard form for very many centuries. The development of Christianity meant that some new virtues were recognised – notably charity, which, often under its secular title of 'benevolence' or 'beneficence', has held a high place ever since. In the eighteenth century Hume, for instance, chose to present the moral ideas of his day by undertaking an analysis of the idea of personal merit, which he took to consist in the possession of various qualities of character, some of which were immediately agreeable and others useful either to their possessors or other people. As late as the end of the nineteenth century, Sidgwick arranged his very careful description of common-sense moral opinions under the headings of the names of the virtues. He was conscious that there was some artificiality in this, and of course now the word 'virtue' no longer figures in our active vocabularies, though inevitably we continue to think some dispositions morally admirable and others not.

Another way of thinking of the moral beliefs of a society is as a code of rules. This juridical conception of morality is congenial to the Judaeo-Christian religious tradition, at any rate on some interpretations. God is cast for the role of moral legislator, and the Church promulgates and perhaps even enforces the divine law. The rule approach to morality also ties in with secular, or secularisable, notions of natural law according to which moral rules can be worked out by natural reasoning without the assistance of divine revelation. Clarke and Price are prominent among the older British moral philosophers who take a rule view of morality. Among twentieth-century moral philosophers Ross and Raphael have chosen to present the facts of morality in this way.

There are genuine differenes, in form as well as content, among the moral beliefs of different societies. That the ancient Greeks seem not to have conceived morality in terms of rules, reveals something of the difference between their way of life and that of, say, seventeenth-century England. On the other hand it is clear that, up to a point, the same moral data can be presented in different ways. But above all it is obvious that much of the detail of morality is not captured in the very general, schematic, descriptions common in moral philosophy. Even when examples of allegedly 'concrete' moral problems are given, they are notoriously stylised, and tend in fact to be copied by one writer from another.

The phenomena of morality are extremely complex and diverse and, while the philosophical impulse to simplify and systematise is not necessarily vicious, it is important to cultivate a capacity to see behind the virtues, rules, examples of moral philosophy, the realities of the moral life. Reading in sociology and anthropology is very helpful here. So is novel reading.

Even when the raw data of morality have been reduced to some sort of order, the need has frequently been felt for further systematisation. The understanding rebels at a merely random list of virtues or a set of quite unrelated obligations or rules. Aristotle thought that the many virtues all involved the exercise of practical wisdom, and Hume, as already noticed, thought morally admirable qualities could be generally described as qualities pleasing or useful to the possessor or others. Where morality is conceived as a matter of rules, it has correspondingly often been thought possible to represent the many rules accepted in a society as derivable from one or a few fundamental rules. The PRINCIPLE OF UTILITY – that actions are right in proportion as they produce happiness, wrong as they produce the reverse of happiness (to follow Mill's formulation) – is a popular candidate for the post of supreme moral principle. The rule that promises should be kept may be held to follow from it to the extent that life in a community in which this rule is kept is likelier to be happier than one in which it is not. One can also, by appeal to the principle of utility, hope to explain the limits to the authority of the promise keeping rule – in the, possibly rare, cases when keeping a promise would produce more unhappiness for everybody concerned than breaking it, it will be right to break it. Kant's CATEGORICAL IMPERATIVE – that one ought to act on maxims that one can will to be universal laws (that is, roughly, that one would be prepared to see everybody else act upon in similar circumstances) – is an alternative suggestion for the supreme principle of morality. It fits some cases well enough: the liar is willing to deceive others, but presumably does not want them to deceive him.

None of the many attempts to formulate a single, fundamental moral principle has met with generally recognised success. Perhaps not surprisingly in view of the extreme variousness of the circumstances in which moral judgements are made. All the same, such very general principles as Mill's or Kant's are not simply the arbitrary invention of philosophers. They embody high-level values – welfare (the principle of utility), justice (the categorical imperative) – that are recognised by quite unphilosophical moralists. It is, in fact, possible to discern in the thinking of all developed societies different levels of moral belief. There are more general ideas in the light of which more particular ones, the detailed rules of conduct, can be justified or criticised. Such differences of level make moral reasoning and argument possible and are crucial for the understanding of moral change and moral differences among cultures.

The fact of moral diversity – different rules of conduct, different values – among cultures, and for that matter among sub-groups within a single complex culture, is the greatest obstacle to seeing morality as a rational affair. We hanker for moral ABSO-LUTES, but we suspect or fear that RELATIVISM is nearer the mark. The truth is, however, that there is no simple inference from the fact of moral diversity to a moral relativism in which anything goes, according to which we are forced to allow that, if the Romans or the Andaman Islanders do it, it must be right *for them*. Marital arrangements, property rules, conventions concerning fair play and the keeping of faith vary greatly from culture to culture. But it is a matter for investigation, not assumption or speculation, how far this diversity is merely arbitrary, without rhyme or reason, and how far it results from the fact that the realisation of the same high-level values will require different measures in different social circumstances. Differences of detailed moral belief that correspond to differences in circumstances testify to the rationality, not the irrationality, of morality. So do changes in moral belief that are relatable to other social changes. It would be no tribute to the rationality of morality if our sexual code, for instance, was in no way affected by developments in contraception, by the economic emancipation of women and young people. Simple-minded absolutism, if it is the view that detailed rules can be formulated which will be valid everywhere and always, can hardly be defended. But reflection on the way in which high-level values may persist through moral diversity and moral change, may convince the more open-minded would-be absolutist that the essence of what he wants to defend is still secure.

In the course of this section I have made certain observations about morality. I have not, however, tried to say exactly what it is. Definitions, if they came at all, come at the end, not the beginning of philosophy books. The questions that will be considered below are not precise queries about some exactly delimited subject matter. Their point is often that they force us to reflect upon their subject matter. We do not need to know what morality is before we can ask them, but in trying to answer them we ought to be able to improve our understanding of it.

PLAN OF THE BOOK

The remainder of the book falls into three parts. Chapters 2 to 4 consider certain problems that arise *within* morality, at points where our moral ideas seem obscure and contradictory. The next two chapters are different and concern questions *about* morality, notably questions about the logical status of moral judgements and the distinction between fact and value. The final part of the book, chapter 7, aims to apply some of the findings of the earlier parts to questions about the *external* relations of morality.

SUMMARY

Moral philosophy is the conceptual study of morality, to be distinguished both from scientific or factual enquiry and from first order moralising.

The morality of a society may consist in the recognition of certain virtues and/or of certain rules of conduct. In the interests of systematisation, philosophers have sought common factors among virtues, or tried to present a variety of moral rules as consequences of such fundamental rules as the principle of utility or the categorical imperative. More and less general levels may be distinguished in moral beliefs. This is crucial for the understanding of moral arguments and the absolutist/relativistic dispute about moral diversity and change.

NOTE

1. *Morals and ethics.* I have distinguished first order morality from moral philosophy, the second order study of it. 'ETHICS' is sometimes recommended as a synonym for 'moral philosophy', in which case the

morality/moral philosophy distinction appears as a distinction between morality (or morals) and ethics. This might be a convenient usage (though it leads to the, to my mind, disagreeable use of 'ethicist' for 'moral philosopher'), but there is no hope of its general adoption. 'Ethics' is very commonly employed at the first order level, especially in phrases like 'business ethics', 'professional ethics'. 'Ethics' is also used in some philosophical writings for the more reflective or general sort of first order moralising. In this application it may be qualified as 'normative ethics', in which case moral philosophy proper will be called ethical analysis or meta-ethics. The morals/ethics distinction is very important, but it is not at all clear when the words are used without explanation which distinction is intended. Purely terminological questions are, of course, only important because of their power to obscure and mislead.

FURTHER READING

An understanding of the nature of moral philosophy is best obtained, not from general pronouncements, but from reading representative works, e.g. Hare (18)* and/or (19). Warnock's brief survey (69) should be useful, too. A rather narrow, though influential, view of the scope of moral philosophy can be found in Ayer (2, chapter 6).

'Classics' of moral philosophy include: Plato (51), though the shorter (50) has some advantages; Aristotle (1) is hard going for beginners; Butler (9), Hume (25), Mill (40) and Kant (29) – the latter, as always, very hard reading.

Relevant psychological studies include Piaget (49), Freud (16). See also Flügel (15) and Ginsberg (17).

MacIntyre (37) aims to bring out relationships between developments in moral philosophy and developments in morality. Hart (20, chapter 8) discusses morality and law, Baier (4, chapters 1 and 5) morality and custom. On morality and politics see Carritt (10).

Sidgwick (62), though not exciting reading, has some claim to be considered one of the best works on moral philosophy in English.

On rule conceptions of morality see extracts from Clarke and Price in Selby-Bigge (61), Ross (58 or 59), Raphael (56).

On the moralities of other cultures Mead (38) is interesting and readable, as is MacBeath (36). Brandt (7) and Ladd (32) are very elaborate and detailed studies.

On the principle of utility, see Mill (40), on the categorical imperative, Kant (29, especially section 2).

On absolutism and relativism, see Ginsberg (17) and the readings in Brandt (81).

* Numbers in parentheses refer to Bibliography, pages 111 ff.

2 Conflicts of Duty

MORAL CONFLICT

Some people are led to philosophy by a quite general desire to understand, others are forced into it by contradictions they encounter in some fields of special concern. Kant was driven to write his elaborate *Critique of Pure Reason* (28) by antinomies concerning the infinitude or otherwise of the world in space and time, causation and freedom, atheism and theism. The need to resolve paradoxes has been an important incentive in the philosophy of mathematics and logic. Conflicting duties are a point of strain within first-order morality which cannot be eased without recourse to theory.

There are several sorts of moral conflict. We may come into conflict with other people over what ought to be done. Or we may be in conflict within ourselves to the extent that we cannot make up our minds what we ought to do. Or again, even though we may be quite clear what we morally speaking ought to do, this may conflict with what from other points of view we most want to do. Such conflicts may be very difficult to resolve and, practically speaking, they may be very painful and worrying, but they are not worrying in the way that a conflict of duties is. For here there appears to be, not just conflict over what the requirements of morality are or whether they should prevail over considerations of other sorts, but a conflict between two equally valid moral requirements. This is disturbingly like finding oneself believing that something both is and is not the case.

Common examples of conflicting duties concern truth telling and saving life or avoiding distress. Kant, in a notorious passage, considers whether one may tell a lie (to a homicidal maniac about his intended victim's whereabouts) in order to save a life, and

B

people who have care of the dangerously sick sometimes wonder whether to tell them the truth about their condition or to keep them happy with optimistic lies. Such cases are obviously possible, but it may be doubted whether they are often, or ever, genuinely conflicts of equally valid moral requirements. Kant surely makes extraordinarily heavy weather over lying to save a life (most of us would doubtless very readily do so), and it may be that in actual cases there will normally be some special feature which will determine which of the conflicting duties is the more important. There do, however, seem to be some types of case in which conflict is less easily resolved – as when, for example, it is necessary to choose between loyalty to friends or benefactors and loyalty to country or professional code, or when one is being held to a solemn undertaking given in all good faith which one has come to think it would be disastrous to carry out.

It is usual to describe such conflicts as conflicts of *duty*, but in fact the problem is not specific to duty. There may be conflicts in situations in which it would not be natural to talk of duty at all. We frequently speak of moral obligations, of what ought to be done, or of what it would be good or desirable to do, in contexts in which the word 'duty' would be inappropriate. Moral philosophers sometimes use 'duty' very widely to cover all sorts of moral requirement, but this is contrary to usage and potentially misleading. Moore suggested that 'duty' tended to be used in cases where the action prescribed (or prohibited) was one we are very strongly tempted to omit (or do), and this is part of the story, though there can be pleasant duties.[1] The more important point seems to be that we reserve 'duty' for situations and people in which and for whom there are definite rules of conduct. Thus we speak of a soldier's or policeman's duty, of the duties of parents, teachers, etc., but not so happily of moral duties unless we think that morality, too, is a matter of rules and regulations (cf. [2]).

It is easy to see why, *if* moral conflicts arise, they will be peculiarly worrying. (It is for much the same reasons that it is sometimes denied that they can or must arise.) They are worrying because the agent seems, impossibly, to be required both to do and not to do. The harder he tries to fulfil one requirement, the less he can hope to fulfil the other. The more he tries to do as he ought, the less he can succeed. It is a trap from which there is no way out. Whatever one does must be wrong. It is tempting to suppose that the nature of morality is such that it is always possible, if only by heroic effort, to avoid incurring moral censure – but not, it seems, in a conflict situation.

One way of avoiding this conclusion, without denying that conflicts can arise, is to maintain that when they do it is the agent's own fault. Once in he cannot avoid doing wrong, but he could have avoided getting in. He need not have made incompatible promises, he should have realised when he made an unconditional offer of support to a friend that he was committing himself to some possibly very dubious courses of action. And so on. Such possiblities are obviously real enough. We often do get into conflict situations through our own fault, and the element of contradictoriness, is, so to say, in us rather than morality. It is worth emphasising this, but it is not the whole truth. In the first place, even if it is in a way always the agent's *fault* that he undertakes to meet conflicting requirements, the fault will not always be what is normally regarded as a *moral* one. I may genuinely have thought I could attend a meeting in London at 10 a.m. and another in York at 2 p.m. I might have checked and double checked the trains, left sufficient time for taxis, and so on. It can hardly be held to be my fault that the railway line is swept away by floods, or the service interrupted by a lightning strike. And even if I had actually made a mistake, say in reading the timetable, and not just been unlucky, such *intellectual* errors are not usually held to be culpable. Moral conflicts frequently arise because two types of moral requirement, which are quite independent of one another, cannot both be met in a particular case. There is no way of guaranteeing absolutely that such conflicts will never arise, or of infallibly predicting the case in which they will.

But it has been denied that they can arise, and, while it might seem that there is an element of wilful paradox here, it is all the same instructive to consider on what the denial is based. 'Ought' implies 'can', i.e. it is of the nature of a moral requirement that it should be possible to carry it out. Hence, 'cannot' implies 'It is not the case that one ought' – if something cannot be done, it is not morally requisite that it should be. A conflict situation is one in which it seems that one ought both to do *A* and to do *B* even though one cannot do them both. But if one really cannot, then it cannot be that one ought. This line of thought lies behind Kant's pronouncement that, although there can be conflicting *grounds* of obligation (duty), there cannot strictly be conflicting *obligations*. That *A* is a friend is a ground for thinking we ought to help him, that he is, say, selling official secrets to a foreign embassy is a ground for holding we ought to denounce him (i.e. *not* help him). But there are not *two* obligations here, because we cannot discharge both. We do not arrive at an obligation proper (as distinct from a ground of obligation) until we have made up our minds which we ought to do.

Instead of distinguishing between grounds of obligation and obligations, we might distinguish two ways in which such words as 'obligation', 'duty', 'ought' are used. These may be called the *deliberative* and *verdictive* senses, respectively. It is the former when we say that we ought (in general or other things being equal) to help our friends, denounce traitors, etc. and etc. It is the latter verdictive sense when we say, after having weighed up the pros and cons and made up our minds, that, in this particular situation, we ought to do this or that. In the deliberative sense of 'ought' (in which, of course, it does not imply 'can') there can be conflicts of 'oughts' or duties or obligations: but in the verdictive sense (in which 'ought' does imply 'can') there cannot. To make this deliberative/verdictive distinction does much to resolve the theoretical worry of how, in a conflict situation, we can somehow be obliged to do what we cannot do. It does not, of course, resolve the practical problem of how we are to decide which of the two (deliberative) obligations we ought (verdictively) to carry out. It may also seem that our procedure has been unduly arbitrary – have we not simply invented a distinction in order to solve a puzzle?

There is, however, another not unrelated distinction which is real enough. This is the distinction between what is *held*, by some individual, group, or people generally, *to be* an obligation or duty and what *is* an obligation or duty. For instance, if I am a pacifist, I might say that it is held to be a duty to fight for one's country but that it is really a duty to refuse to do so. (This use of 'really' need not carry 'objectivist' implications – see below for a discussion of OBJECTIVISM.) For the non-pacifist, of course, the distinction between what is held to be and what is a duty (or obligation) will not be important in this particular case, and in so far as most of us most of the time go along with the moral beliefs of our fellows, it will frequently not seem important to us. It may therefore be that we shall often use 'ought', 'obligation' and 'duty' for two different purposes. One is to report the moral views of our society, which we will often share, the other is to express our personal moral conviction. Hare has termed the former use of 'ought', 'obligation', etc. or rather the use of 'ought', etc. exclusively for the former purpose, the 'inverted commas' use – the idea being that 'ought' is here quoted rather than used.[3] (This involves treating the 'ought' of personal conviction, which is closely akin to the verdictive 'ought' of the previous paragraph, as the *primary* use of 'ought'.) It is very clear indeed that inverted commas 'oughts' may conflict: that is to say, that the rules of any particular code – the laws of the land, the Queen's regulations, the rules of football or chess – may conflict in the sense that following one will lead to disobeying another. Any social rules, customs, practices may conflict in this way. Is there any reason why the same should not be true of moral rules? (If they are some sort of social rules, then it will be, if not, then perhaps they are not social rules.) I think that we feel some reluctance to say this of morality. Moral rules express requirements that we have to follow come what may. It is natural to identify the moral 'ought' with the verdictive 'ought', the 'ought' that implies 'can', the ought of personal conviction. It does not seem that we can regard moral rules as a sort of, possibly conflicting, social rules.

In the next section we shall consider whether there is any possibility of so conceiving moral rules that conflicts cannot occur.

THE OBLIGATORY AND THE DESIRABLE

One way of dealing with conflicting moral rules rests on the traditional distinction between duties of *perfect* and duties of *imperfect* obligation. In more nearly contemporary language this might be called the distinction between the *obligatory* and the *desirable*. There are various ways in which it may be drawn, but it is probably best to begin by illustrating it with examples.

Duties to tell the truth, keep promises, pay debts are typically perfect: duties of prudence (having regard to one's own welfare) and beneficence (promoting other people's welfare) typically imperfect. Given such a distinction, it might be hoped that conflicts of equal duties could be avoided by resolving that in every conflict the perfect duty was to be preferred to the imperfect, (the desirable set aside in favour of the obligatory). As we shall see, it may be held that conflicts among imperfect duties are unworrying and that conflicts among perfect duties will not occur.

The success of this manoeuvre depends on the way the perfect/ imperfect distinction is drawn.

In the first place, it may be noticed that the perfect duties of truth telling and debt paying are determinate in a way the imperfect duties are not. The truth is to be told in every single case. Every single lie counts as a violation of the duty. But we cannot be required to help every single person who is in need. Obviously nobody could, and consequently we do not violate the imperfect duty of promoting welfare simply by failing to help a particular individual. There is no discretion where perfect duties are concerned, but we can to some extent choose how our imperfect duties are to be discharged. (We ought to support some good cause, but which is up to us.) It is in this way that one can interpret the Kantian observation that perfect duties are strict while imperfect duties leave some latitude for inclination. One can also see why it is sometimes said that perfect duties lend themselves to being enforced by law while imperfect ones do not. Offences must be precisely defined and laws consequently prescribe only determinate acts. (This is sometimes presented as a logical point following from the nature – the definition – of law: but it really expresses a demand for a certain sort of legal system.)

There is another ground of difference between perfect and imperfect duties, the obligatory and the desirable. With the former, but not the latter, there will always be some particular individual who has a correlative right. If I owe you money (have a duty to pay you), you have a right to be paid. But, it may plausibly be suggested, we would not say that you in particular had a right to be helped simply because I have an imperfect duty to help people. In a sense, of course, I ought to help you, but you cannot claim as of right that I should. I may legitimately decide to exercise my charity elsewhere.

A further point which connects with the previous one is that perfect duties may be regarded as defining the moral minimum, that which cannot be omitted without fault even though the performance of it does not deserve a great deal of credit. Performing imperfect duties, however, goes beyond the minimum and so earns merit. You can do more or less in the way of carrying out imperfect duties, whereas with perfect duties you either discharge them or you do not.

It is apparent that to think in terms of a distinction between perfect and imperfect duties is to conceive morality as a formal code. In such a code there could be a perfectly precise distinction, but the morality most of us recognise is not at all like this and, while there may be some possibility of making a distinction, there is no settling the exact nature of it. Probably it is better to think in terms of a set of nearly coincident distinctions than of one fundamental one.

But what about the main issue? Can conflicts of duty be resolved in this way? The line of thought is plain. Any particular act (e.g. helping an individual) which falls under an imperfect duty can be omitted without fault. It can, therefore, be omitted when it conflicts with a perfect duty. It is of the nature of imperfect duties to admit to postponement, of perfect duties not to. It is, incidentally, for this reason that conflicts between two imperfect duties present no problem.

Against this, however, it may be wondered whether we are in fact always prepared to prefer a perfect to an imperfect duty. This is, of course, a question of moral judgement on which people may differ. But most of us frequently feel it right to tell lies, break promises, repudiate debts in the interests of helping other people. (We sometimes partially conceal this by describing the lies we think legitimate as white lies or even harmless or necessary deceptions. Promises that need breaking can be redescribed as unwise undertakings – there is a great deal of scope here.) The situation must not be over-simplified. We also often condemn people for neglecting their perfect duties (the obligatory) for their imperfect ones (the desirable), e.g. by using money needed to pay their bills for Oxfam. We do seem to accord some priority to perfect duties, but not by any means in every case. The truth seems to be that we think that some duties are more important than others – roughly on a scale determined by the amount of clearly foreseeable harm ignoring them would cause – and, without paying too much attention to the type of duty involved, where there is a conflict we prefer the more important to the less.

There remains the possibility of conflict among perfect duties themselves. On the face of it this is possible. We may, for instance, make promises we cannot simultaneously fulfil, or, having promised to keep some information secret, find that we can do so only by telling a lie.

We have already held that it is not plausible to maintain that conflicts of, possibly equal, perfect duties arise only through the agent's fault. A different sort of point that is often made in this connection is that perfect duties, being *negative* (shalt *nots* rather than shalts), cannot properly speaking conflict with one another. It is indeed quite plausible to represent perfect duties as negative, as prohibitions rather than positive prescriptions. The duty to tell the truth is really the duty *not* to lie. Then there are the duties *not* to break promises, *not* to disregard debts. The importance of this lies in the fact that, while there never can be an absolute guarantee that it will be possible to obey both of two positive prescriptions, there is a sense in which *any* two prohibitions can be obeyed. Whatever the two acts may be, it will always be possible to omit (not to do) both of them. Consider the question of deceiving a would-be murderer about the whereabouts of his victim (Kant's example, which was mentioned towards the beginning of this chapter). Here the conflict is presumably between the duty not to kill and the duty not to lie. The assumption is that if we do not lie the victim will be killed, but we can still obey both prohibitions. It may very well be that the victim is killed because we have not lied – but he will not have been killed by *us*, *we* will not have violated any prohibition. Another case often discussed in this connection is one on which an obstetrician has to choose between preserving the life of a mother and the life of her unborn child. It may very well be impossible to save both lives, but it does not follow that the obstetrician must therefore take one of them. If he decides not to kill the child the mother may die, but he will not have killed her – at worst, he allowed her to die. One may feel, and most non-Roman Catholic moralists do feel, that the distinction between killing and allowing to die is not here of moral significance – that it is as bad, or worse, to let the mother die as it would be to kill the child in order to save her. Nevertheless it is clear that, *if* we are prepared both to regard perfect duties as negative and to regard the act/omission (doing and letting happen) distinction as morally significant, *then* we have no need to worry about the possibility of perfect duties conflicting. A more general moral is that, if we want to recognise some moral absolutes (moral requirements that *never* can be set aside), we shall have to make them prohibitions and give moral weight to the act/omission distinction.

I do not argue that the act/omission distinction is never morally significant, that permitting something to happen when one could prevent it is always morally speaking tantamount to doing it. Whether it is significant or not seems to me to depend on considerations that vary from case to case. It follows that I must allow that perfect duties can conflict, and that I must be very wary of moral absolutes.

PRIMA FACIE DUTIES

With some artificiality, duties or obligations can be classified under a few general headings. There are various ways in which this can be done, but a well known one is that of Ross (58, and compare Raphael (56)). Ross recognises six categories: first are duties of fidelity and reparation; second, duties of gratitude; third, those of justice; fourth, beneficence; fifth, self-improvement (see next chapter); and sixth, non-maleficence, which, as the duty of not injuring others, is distinguished from beneficence, the duty of positively doing good to them. Manifestly there could be conflicts between duties of the different types, and it would, therefore, be incoherent to regard them all as *strict* duties, duties which had to be performed without any qualification or abatement. Accordingly, Ross proposed that they should be regarded as *prima facie* duties only, that is to say that, for instance, the rule of truth telling (which comes under the head of fidelity) should be regarded as having only conditional force. It categorically obliges one not to lie only if no other rule (say of non-maleficence) applies to the situation. Where there are two conflicting rules bearing upon a situation, it is necessary to balance the one against the other in order to discover where *strict* duty lies, i.e. what actually ought to be done. The rules of *prima facie* duty specify considerations which are relevant, but not decisive in determining strict duty. (The *prima facie*/strict duty distinction resembles that made in the first section of this chapter between the deliberative and verdictive 'oughts'.)

Ross was anxious to present moral rules as self-evident truths with the same sort of status as geometrical axioms. This they could hardly be if they were rules of strict duty – it cannot be self-evident that one both should and should not keep a promise in a situation in which keeping the promise would cause injury. But perhaps it could be self-evident *both* that an act's being the keeping of a promise was a reason for doing it *and* that its involving injury for someone was a reason for not doing it. We are not, at present, concerned with the question whether any moral rule can be self-evident (chapter 5, pages 54–7 and 64–71 but only with the realism, or otherwise, truth or falsity to actual moral thinking, of Ross's way of regarding moral rules.

It is undeniable that all moralists would accept the very general considerations he sets out as relevant to the question of what ought to be done. Furthermore, it seems probable that no one consideration is held to be invariably decisive, not even those of non-maleficence and beneficence, which together amount to something close to the principle of utility mentioned in the previous chapter (page 13). It was one of Ross's central contentions that the moral consciousness was not uniformly utilitarian. Indeed he thought it impossible to make any general statement about the relative weights to be attached to his several rules, except that it was more important to avoid inflicting injury (non-maleficence) than to confer benefits (beneficence). This may seem a rather un-enterprising judgement, but it is not therefore untrue to ordinary moral thinking. Ross is perhaps more successful than most moral philosophers in resisting the impulse to tidy up the raw data of morality.

Other writers, who start with a view of moral phenomena not unlike Ross's (e.g. Toulmin and Baier), try to provide more guidance than he does for resolving conflicts of *prima facie* duties. One way is to pick out the rules of non-maleficence and ben-ficence and treat them as rules of a higher order – rules not for judging actions, but for judging rules. Such rules as that of promise keeping can, with considerable plausibility, be represented as rules of which the widespread observance reduces friction and promotes harmony in society. In a particular case, keeping such a rule may do more harm than good, but more good will result on the whole if the rules are generally kept than if they are generally, or even frequently, disregarded. This sort of view resembles UTILITARIANISM, except that the utilitarian test (the principle of utility) is applied not to particular actions, but rather to rules. It is, therefore, sometimes referred to as *rule-* as opposed to *act-*utilitarianism. In act-utilitarianism, justification is always on the one level – the question is always, which of the acts open to us in the circumstances will most promote welfare? For rule-utilitarianism it is a two-stage affair. In the first instance, one asks whether a proposed act is required or forbidden by an accepted moral rule. The second stage is to ask whether the rule is one of which the observance promotes welfare. In many cases there will be no occasion to pass beyond the first stage of justification, the act in question will be clearly prescribed or prohibited by *one* social rule. But there will be cases in which two rules have differ-ent implications, and in these there must be appeal to the higher order principle in order to decide between them.

On the face of it, rule-utilitarianism is an attractive compromise between the inconclusive, but possibly accurately reported, set of *prima facie* duties of Ross and full-blown act-utilitarianism. There has been a great deal of discussion of rule-utilitarianism in recent years and an extensive literature has grown up. There are some internal difficulties in rule-utilitarianism, some uncertainties about formulation, and some room for doubt whether it is, when carefully set out, really different from act-utilitarianism. There is also disagreement as to which of the classical utilitarians were rule- and which act-utilitarians – Mill's position, in this respect as in many others, is by no means clear.

Rule-utilitarianism is a good illustration of the relation between moral philosophy and morality. It is not a straightforward description of the 'moral facts', but neither is it a mere invention of philosophers. It begins with considerations which are recognised by all moralists and proceeds to generalise and systematise them. It is neither simple truth nor arbitrary fiction, but a development from, and possible improvement upon, accepted ideas.

Moral philosophy, even at the quasi-descriptive level we are considering, still reacts with its subject-matter. It has sometimes been thought that philosophers could, by analysing accepted moral beliefs, extract principles which they could then *prove* and thus supply a philosophical foundation for morality. (This seems to be Kant's programme in his *Groundwork* (29).) We shall see, however, in chapter 5 that this cannot be done. But, even though proofs are not available, there is still the possibility of moral philosophy having a beneficial effect on its subject-matter.

SUMMARY

It appears that duties or other moral requirements may conflict in the sense that it is impossible for an agent to carry out both. Such conflicts are sometimes, but not always, the agent's fault, e.g. because he made foreseeably incompatible promises. Sometimes it is denied that there can be a conflict of moral requirements on the grounds that it is of the nature of a moral requirement that it can be carried out – 'ought' implies 'can'. Distinguish the deliberative and verdictive senses of 'ought'. Another distinction is between the 'ought' which reports the moral conviction of some group (the 'inverted commas' sense) and the 'ought' of personal conviction. It is doubtful whether moral requirements can be identified with social rules.

The distinction between perfect and imperfect duties as a means of resolving conflicts of moral rules is considered. Perfect duties are determinate and carry correlative rights in particular individuals, imperfect duties are neither. When there is conflict it is doubtful, however, whether most people are willing always to prefer the perfect duty. Moreover, perfect duties themselves may conflict unless they are regarded as negative and an act/omission distinction insisted on. Moral absolutes need to be so conceived.

Ross's view that moral rules should be regarded as rules of *prima facie* rather than strict duty (compare the distinction between the deliberative and verdictive 'ought'). Possibly *both* unsatisfying *and* a faithful reflection of ordinary moral thinking. Rule-utilitarianism as a defensible extension of moral thinking. The relationship between moral philosophy and its subject matter.

NOTES

1. Moore (43), page 218.
2. Hare (18), page 162.
3. Hare (18), pages 121-6.

FURTHER READING

On conflicts of duty, see Raphael (56, chapter 7), also Atkinson and Williams (74). On the use of the word 'duty', see Whiteley (80). Note Kant's essay, 'The Supposed Right to Tell a Lie from Benevolent Motives' (30). Hare (19, chapter 4), is a useful discussion of 'ought' and 'can'. Hare (18, see index) should be consulted for the 'inverted commas' sense of 'ought'.

Kant makes some use of the distinction between perfect and imperfect duties in his *Groundwork* (29, section 2). On the correlativity of rights and duties, see Ross (58, chapter 2, appendix 1) and Raphael (56, chapter 4, section 2).

For the distinction between strict and *prima facie* duties, see Ross (58, chapter 2). Baier (4) and Toulmin (68), writing in a different philosophical framework, take a somewhat similar view of first-order morality. On act and rule-utilitarianism there is an enormous literature; Brandt (8, chapter 15) is a good source. Lyons (34) is a scholarly, but possibly difficult, treatment of the distinction. On Mill's view, see Urmson and Mabbott (both in Foot 82).

3 Oneself and Others

In this chapter, as in the previous one, we shall be dealing with morality at a point of conceptual strain. We have seen how it can appear both that moral requirements conflict and that it is of their nature that they should not. Somewhat similarly, though this is a less worrying perplexity, it may seem that people both can and cannot have duties to themselves.

On the one side there is the fact that duties have traditionally been classified under two or three heads: as duties to oneself (e.g. Ross's duties of self-improvement); to other people; and perhaps also to God. (Duties to God will not be considered here – most of the difficulties about them arise from difficulties about God.) On the other side may be cited the *quasi-contractual* character of duty, and the (possibly) essentially *other-regarding* (utilitarian) character of morality.

The contractual character of duty is the clearer though less important point. Some at least, of our duties derive from explicit or implicit agreements with other people. I borrow money and undertake to pay it back, or you tell me something in confidence and I give you to understand that I will not divulge it. Now, in so far as duties are contractual, they will be *to* somebody, and generally speaking that somebody will be at liberty to release one from discharging the duty. You can release me from my promises to you, but unless and until you do release me I am bound by them. My having a duty (being under an obligation), it may well be felt, consists in my being thus bound. So there hardly can be duties to oneself, because one cannot be bound by oneself. I may indeed speak figuratively of promising myself this or that, but a bond from which I can release myself at will does not oblige. There is no promise when promisor and promisee are the same person.

But how, in face of this, has it come about that people have recognised duties to oneself? By way of an answer it might be said that the 'to' in 'duty *to* so and so' is ambiguous as between 'owed to' and 'in respect of'. The next point is that the person to whom the duty is owed may or may not be the same as the person in respect of whom it has to be carried out. When I am in your debt, you are both the person to whom I am under an obligation and the person in respect of whom it has to be discharged (it is you to whom the money has to be paid). But, if I have undertaken to supervise the education of your children while you are overseas, then I owe the duty to you but the activity it requires of me is in respect of your children. Only you, not your children, can release me from the duty: but the duty is to see to their education, not yours.

With the aid of this distinction, it is not difficult to resolve some of the difficulty in the idea of a duty to oneself. It can be allowed that there is no possibility of a duty being owed to oneself, while there very well could be duties owed to others which involve actions relating to oneself. For instance, suicide may be condemned as a breach of duty respecting oneself but owed to others, the suicide being thought of as abdicating his responsibilities to family or country. There would be a complete solution to the problem of duties to oneself if all duties regarding oneself could be regarded as derivative from duties to other people. The derivative duties would be to make and keep oneself capable of discharging duties to others by attending to one's health, education, finance, and so on. Even Kant, who very sharply distinguished the requirements of PRUDENCE (which he conceived as a matter of promoting one's own happiness) from those of morality proper, thought that there was a secondary duty to observe the requirements of prudence in order to make it easier to obey the moral law proper.

It is, however, doubtful whether everything that Ross would have brought under duties of self-improvement can be regarded as derivative from duties to others. And there is a good deal still to discuss before it is reasonable to form an opinion how far morality is an other-regarding affair.

MORALITY AND PRUDENCE

Prudence is distinguished from morality by its object. It is regard for one's own happiness or welfare, whereas morality almost certainly is not that (though there have been ETHICAL EGOISTS), but is rather a concern for the welfare of others (ETHICAL ALTRUISM) or of everybody, including therefore oneself (ETHICAL NEUTRALISM). Prudence has, it is true, often been classed as virtue, i.e. a *morally* admirable quality, but this may be partly because it is not always conceived with sufficient distinctness, and sometimes because it has been supposed (e.g. by Butler and many of the earlier utilitarians) that promoting one's own happiness or welfare will, as a matter of fact, lead to the performance of actions that will promote the happiness or welfare of everybody.

Perhaps it does not matter very much whether prudence is regarded as distinct from morality or only as a distinct department within it. More important is the question whether it is at least distinct. The word, certainly, is no longer much used, but there does seem to be widespread recognition of what would once have been called the requirements of prudence. People are enjoined not to smoke in order to avoid lung cancer, to work for their examinations, to live within their incomes, to make provision for possible illness and unemployment. Up to a point these are like moral requirements. It is possible to feel tempted to disregard them, to experience conflict and feel guilt, very much as in moral contexts. There seems to be the possibility of conflict between what (prudentially) ought to be done and what is wanted, and this in spite of the facts that the obligations of prudence are essentially to do what is necessary to get what one wants (or to avoid what must not be done if one is not to get what one does not want), and that the obligations are therefore not incumbent on anyone who does not want (or wants to avoid) the end-results in question.

Prudence is neither simply a matter of going for what one wants nor simply a matter of subordinating one's wants to those of others (or to the requirements of morality, if that is different). It is rather the subordinating of occasional and less important wants to long-term, fundamental ones. To the extent that prudence involves disregarding certain wants it resembles morality, but in so far as this is done for the sake of other wants (albeit long-term, fundamental ones) it differs from it. Prudence, so long as there are no errors of calculation, will always pay the individual, morality need not. It is significant that we tend to regard the imprudent man as irrational or foolish rather than immoral, and that we do not think immorality necessarily irrational. On occasion, to say the least, it pays. Questions about rationality of morality seem to arise once it is distinguished from prudence. One of the main problems of Plato's *Republic* (51), whether it is sensible to be just, arises in this way, as does Kant's problem of showing that it is rational to obey the CATEGORICAL IMPERA-TIVES of morality. (Kant thinks it obviously rational to obey HYPOTHETICAL IMPERATIVES, i.e. to do what has to be done to get what one wants, to be prudent. But the imperatives of morality are different. They enjoy people to do or forbear *irrespective* of what they want, and are accordingly termed categorical.)

Some of the difficulty of showing morality to be rational derives from the incoherence of the project. The conception of rationality employed is too often a quite uncritical one, founded upon the concept of prudence. The question about the rationality of morality then amounts to the question whether morality, understood as something different from prudence, is nevertheless the same. And, not surprisingly, no satisfactory answer can ever be found. In this, it resembles another famous unsolved problem of philosophy, the problem of induction (i.e. the problem whether we are justified in basing statements about the future on our experience of the past), which arises because induction is *both* distinguished from deduction *and* yet expected to conform to standards of deductive validity.

SOCIAL MORALITY

We have been trying to think about prudence (regard for one's own welfare) in its distinctness from *morality*, of which we have yet to form a clear conception. It will help to make a fresh start and consider how far morality can be conceived simply as a

c

regard for the welfare of others. John Stuart Mill makes a celebrated distinction in his *Liberty* (40) between actions which affect only the agent himself (*self-regarding* actions) and those which affect other people (*other-regarding* actions). Mill's concern was to confine the law to actions falling into the latter category, but we need to ask the different question: whether morality is similarly restricted in scope, whether it is other-regarding actions alone that come up for moral assessment. If morality really is a purely social affair, the answer will be affirmative.

It is unimportant for the present purpose whether or not a hard distinction can be made between self- and other-regarding actions.

A social conception of morality is implicit in many contemporary discussions of sexual conduct. Many so-called perversions, often considered highly immoral, need not affect other people (non-consenting third parties) – can they therefore sensibly be deemed immoral? Homosexual behaviour in private between consenting adults has recently ceased to be criminal. In the debate that preceded the change in the law, it was scarcely questioned that homosexual behaviour was immoral or sinful. This was no doubt a prudent tactic for those who wanted to change the law, but can the question be shirked? Again, heterosexual behaviour clearly falls within the scope of moral assessment in so far as children may be conceived, but would not the availability of a 100 per cent effective contraceptive transform it into a purely private affair? Of course, some of the activities in question might have social effects of a less obvious kind, but this would need to be established, and on the face of it a purely social approach to morality would remove from its scope many types of behaviour on which moral judgement has traditionally been passed.

It is easy to understand the need for a basic, social morality. There are rules that must be fairly generally observed if social life is to be possible or tolerable. Social morality is not wholly determinate, rules of conduct need not be and have not been the same everywhere and always, but there are areas of human concern where rules of some sort have almost invariably been found necessary, notably, property, sex and aggression. And much of the content of most moral codes can be seen as a response, differing according to a great variety of circumstances, to the need for basic rules of social conduct. Further, the rationale of obeying such rules from the individual's point of view can be readily understood. In particular cases social rules may bear hardly on particular individuals, but, in general, it obviously pays to meet the condition (conformity) for membership of society. Indeed this is much too weak. To belong or not to belong to society is not an effective option for the human individual.

There is little scope for argument about the need for basic, social morality. At most, there can be disagreement about its extent, for instance in the sexual field. But talk of *basic* morality tends to suggest that there may be a non-basic area as well. Is there? It is certainly the case that people sometimes engage in reflection, deliberation and discussion that it is natural to call 'moral' on matters that do not come within the social sphere. Social morality certainly leaves open an area of personal choice, in which morally speaking, we may do as we like. But can this be the whole story? Are there not options which, though of no obvious social concern, are too important to be subject to purely personal whim, as are the colour of cars, the style of clothes, and what is to be eaten and drunk? Some people, indubitably, do frame conceptions of IDEAL patterns of life which they employ to regulate the details of their conduct. Moreover, the demands of such ideals may be more exacting than those of social morality. (Ideals may in fact be an important source of duties to oneself.) The requirements of an ideal are not, like those of social morality, derivative from a system of conduct assessment which is 'objective' in that it reflects the conditions of social existence. They are somehow *self*-imposed, yet not just like the demands of prudence (i.e. not parasitic on our wants and needs), still less are they just wayward whims and fancies. If there be, so to say scope for personal choice and prudence *below* the sphere of social morality, there seems also to be a realm of moral ideals *above* it.

MAKING SENSE OF MORALITY

It is easy to make sense of prudence *narrowly* conceived. To conceive it narrowly is, of course, to simplify it and exclude complications. In the same way, it is easy to make sense of social morality, provided we take no account of its relations with personal choice and ideals. Morality as a whole, however, is resistant to this mode of understanding, by isolation and simplification. It is not just one way of assessing conduct among others. It lays claim to being more fundamental and authoritative. And this, whatever else it may involve, implies a certain comprehensiveness. By all means, as a beginning, let us distinguish morality and prudence, but having done so we still have to allow that, if prudential considerations are important at all, morality must have regard to them. It will not do to stipulate tidily that prudence is concern for one's own welfare, morality for that of other people – it must at least be the case that morality is concern for the welfare of *everybody*, one's own therefore being included. The same applies to ideals. It is helpful to distinguish questions about life ideals from questions of social morality, but in the end it will be necessary somehow to fit together again what has been earlier separated. There is no escaping this. The demands of (some people's) ideals go, not merely *beyond*, but also *against* those of social morality.

We try to pin down morality, to say what it is and what it is not, but it seems to expand as we look at it. This is not accidental, it reflects the practical character of morality that I, at least, take to be essential to it. Morality is practical in that it relates to the questions what we should choose and how we should act. And, consequently, *everything* that bears upon these questions may fall within its scope.

SUMMARY

The difficulty of accepting the idea of duties to oneself derives partly from the quasi-contractual character of duty, and partly from the natural tendency to regard morality as essentially an other-regarding affair.

Morality may provisionally be distinguished from prudence (regard for one's own welfare) as regard for the welfare of *others*, or of *everybody* including oneself. Prudence resembles morality in that it involves some regulation of personal wants, but differs from it in that less important wants are subordinated simply to long-term, fundamental, but still individual, wants. Imprudence is felt to be irrational in a way immorality may not be, and questions about the rationality of morality tend to arise when it is distinguished from prudence. Discussions of the rationality of morality are sometimes vitiated by the employment of an uncritical notion of rationality, closely related to prudence.

How far can morality be conceived as a purely social, other-regarding, affair? Respect for the obligations of social morality is clearly a condition of participation in social life. Social morality, though its content differs in different societies, is 'objective' in that it is founded upon social necessities. But people may regulate their lives by reference to moral ideals which have no such social foundation.

Morality is not simply one mode of conduct assessment among others. It lays claim, in virtue of its practical character, to authority and comprehensiveness. *Everything* that bears upon the question what should be done may fall within its scope.

FURTHER READING

There is a good, recent discussion of duties to oneself in Baier (4, chapter 9). The discussion of duty in Raphael (56, especially chapter 4) is also relevant. Students of moral philosophy are perhaps most likely to come upon the idea of duties to oneself in Kant (29), though it is of course recognised by many other writers.

Kant (29, sections 1 and 2) is notable for a very firm statement of the distinction between prudence and morality (hypothetical and categorical imperatives). Utilitarian writers, e.g. Mill (40), tend to be less clear. Prichard (53, chapter 1) is relevant. There is a chapter on prudence in Carritt (10), and a discussion by Mabbott and Horsburgh (76). Foot is notable among contemporary writers for giving weight to the sort of question raised by Plato about the rationality of justice (see 82, chapter VI).

There are many discussions of the problem of induction, e.g. Hospers (23).

For the distinction between self- and other-regarding actions, see Mill's *Liberty* (40). For discussion of social morality and individual ideals, see Strawson (78) and Hare (19, chapters 8 and 9).

4 Merit and Demerit: Praise and Blame

So far we have been considering morality mainly in its conduct-guiding aspect, as containing prescriptions of how people should behave and of the qualities of character they should seek to acquire. But morality also contains standards for judgement. People are held to acquire merit (are praised) in so far as their conduct measures up to the requirements of morality, and they are held to incur demerit (blamed, held to be culpable or guilty) in so far as their conduct falls short.

The aim of the present chapter is to set out some of the general conditions that have to be satisfied for there to be moral merit and demerit.

First of all, it should be noted that conceptions of merit and demerit are complex. It is not the case that people are invariably praised for fulfilling moral requirements – 'He *only* did his duty' is used to suggest that praise would be excessive – nor are people necessarily blamed when they fail to fulfil them. It seems, in fact, that in addition to notions of what is morally required (what ought or ought not to be done), we have some idea of an expected or average level of performance, and that it is to this latter that reference is made when it is a question of merit and demerit, praise and blame. Thus a person who does what he ought to do in circumstances when most people would have done the same, (when, that is to say, it is easy to do so) is not praised, or not much, though he would have been severely blamed had he not done so. Similarly a person who satisfies moral requirements in exceptionally difficult circumstances may be highly praised, while someone who failed in such circumstances would not be blamed.

Moral merit is earned not simply by doing one's duty, but by exceeding the general level of achievement in the discharge of duty. It is also earned by performing acts which 'go beyond' anything that duty could possibly require – by 'works of SUPER-EROGATION' as they are traditionally called. Examples include such cases as that of the soldier who, instead of taking cover, throws himself on a live grenade and saves his companions' lives at the expense of his own; and many others in which people take enormous risks for the sake of helping others. There are other sorts of cases in which what is exhibited is, not exceptional courage, but rather exceptional endurance, fortitude, tolerance, forgiveness.

These facts are familiar enough, but puzzles have nonetheless been found in them. One way at least in which people acquire moral credit is by doing more than their duty. But if 'duty' expresses the requirement of morality, what goes beyond duty cannot be *morally* required, and, it may be asked, why should anyone be *morally* praised for that? To this question, some writers have responded by trying to represent acts going beyond duty (works of supererogation) as really duties after all. For instance, it may be held that they are duties so difficult of perfor-mance, and hence so unlikely to be performed, that there is no *practical* point in enjoining them on people as duties at all; or, that they are acts which are felt to be duties by the agent, although not generally held to be so by other people. But it is very doubtful whether all acts of supererogation can be fitted into one or other of these categories.

The proper way out of these difficulties lies in making due allowance for the variety of moral requirements – not all of which are duties, nor even strictly speaking *requirements*. There are also conceptions of the desirable and commendable, i.e. of acts which are to be welcomed when they are performed but which people are not expected to perform or blamed for not performing. The importance, from the present point of view, of works of super-erogation and of attempts to refuse them recognition, is that they offer an opportunity to emphasise *both* the complexity of ideas of moral and demerit *and* the tendency among moral philosophers to oversimplify in this area. In the remaining sections of this chapter, some important points will be touched upon, but inevitably others will be missed out. It is more important at this stage to draw attention to issues that require discussion than to try to develop a comprehensive theory. Systematisation in this area almost inevitably means distortion.

CULPABILITY: COMPULSION AND IGNORANCE

Suppose that a person has violated a moral requirement, that he has, for instance, killed or injured a bystander by pulling the trigger of a loaded gun. Under what circumstances would he be held guilty or blamed? Or rather, to ask the more fruitful question, under what circumstances would he *not* be held guilty? According to Aristotle, and very many other writers from his time to ours, EXCULPATORY conditions can be collected under two heads: COMPULSION, when the person could not help what he did because someone jostled him, his hand slipped, the mechanism was faulty etc.; and IGNORANCE, when he did not know that the gun was loaded, that there was anyone in the line of fire, etc.

There is no doubt that exculpations of both these types are sometimes acceptable, but a great many problems arise.

Compulsions

Gross physical compulsion is clearly exculpatory. Nobody is blamed for not doing something he ought if he has been physically prevented from doing so by a stronger person, any more than people are blamed for not discharging their duties when it is physically impossible for them to do so because of illness or injury. There is indeed a difference between compulsions proper, when coercion or obstruction by other individuals is involved, and cases of paralysis or broken limbs, etc.; but as regards culpability the effect is the same. The agent is rendered *incapable* of doing what he ought (or, since 'ought' implies 'can', of doing what, if he could, he ought to do). Physical compulsion does, however, admit of degree, and there is some overlap between compulsions and very severe threats. Threats and physical compulsions are often classed together as exculpating factors but, while there no doubt are threats which are literally irresistible (like the rats which finally break Winston Smith in Orwell's *1984*), there are others which with varying degrees of difficulty can be, and are, resisted. Threats which, though not resisted were resistible, and which therefore do not exculpate, may however constitute grounds of EXCUSE or extenuation. We think less ill of, say a Housing Officer who is blackmailed into allocating a house to an unqualified applicant, than of one who simply responds to a bribe.

It is an interesting speculation why we are readier to entertain the possibility of the irresistible threat than the, on the face of it, equal possibility of the irresistible bribe.

There is a further complication that people are sometimes praised (and to that extent held accountable) for resisting threats so severe that they would not have been blamed (and so, apparently, not held accountable) for succumbing to. It would seem that we ought to be able to determine whether people are accountable or responsible *independently* of what they do, otherwise we shall find ourselves embracing the admittedly not uninviting doctrine that they are responsible only when they act well. Part of the answer here is just that, as we have already noted, liability to praise and blame is related to average performance, and not simply determined by whether or not moral requirements are fulfilled by a particular agent. Another part is that questions about the conditions that have to be met before the possibility of praise or blame arises (i.e. questions about the *logical* conditions for responsibility) need to be distinguished from *moral* questions concerning our entitlement to express praise or blame. Many hold, as a moral not a logical point, that one should not express blame when people have done no worse than one fears one would have done oneself in like circumstances.

Psychological compulsions

These also present some difficulties; Hume, for instance, does not recognise them. For him, a man is accountable for what he does so long as he does not act under external duress. But it is now widely recognised that there are certain mental disorders, such as kleptomania, of which the victims cannot help performing certain sorts of illegal or immoral acts. Such people are by Humean standards accountable and therefore to be blamed or punished for what they do, but this now seems to be unacceptable and the tendency even in courts of law is to regard compulsives as irresponsible – sick no doubt and requiring treatment, but not culpable, not to be blamed or punished. What is the problem here? Why should not psychological compulsions be given exactly the same weight as physical ones? There are at least two difficulties. The first, which is a practical one, is that it is less easy to diagnose cases of psychological than of physical compulsion – the criteria are behavioural, and the behaviour in question has to be observed over a long time. Consequently it seems that it would be fairly easy for people to escape the consequences of their misdeeds by feigning mental disorders, and hence that to allow such disorders to exculpate would weaken the deterrent effectiveness of the law. This sort of consideration does not necessarily carry over from legal to moral culpability, but in fact it does encourage some resistance to psychological compulsions being regarded as morally exculpatory. If people are to be deemed irresponsible on such elusive grounds, how can we be sure that anyone ever is responsible? And this is, in effect, the second, more theoretical difficulty. Compulsive behaviour shades off into 'normal' behaviour by imperceptible degrees. Physical compulsions and threats admit of degree, but much of the time most of us are not subject to either. Nor, mostly, are we incapable of doing as we should because of physical illness or injury. But how can we ever know that we or others are free from psychological compulsion? Is not the admission of psychological compulsion the first step towards denying that anybody is accountable for anything he does?

I think that it is possible to give weight to psychological compulsions without compromising our idea of accountability. The limits of the concept of psychological compulsion are indefinite, but it does not follow that there are no limits. The difficulty of deciding exactly where a boundary should run does not, here as elsewhere, make it impossible to draw a distinction. But at this point, the particular problem of psychological compulsion merges with the much more general doubt whether human actions can be in any way RESPONSIBLE (voluntary or free) when it is determined, or caused, by factors which are ultimately beyond the agents' control. This is the celebrated problem of free-will, of FREEDOM and DETERMINISM, for many the major obstacle to making sense of morality. It is widely thought, not only that determinism is incompatible with moral freedom and responsibility, but that the case for determinism has been greatly strengthened by the development of science, and particularly psychological science.

I do not myself think that determinism, in any remotely credible form, is a severe threat to our notions of responsibility and freedom. (There are serious problems of formulation to be solved before we reach the question whether there is any reason to think any sort of determinism true.) But discussion of this matter will be postponed to chapter 7, on the ground that the problem is less one that arises *within* morality than one that arises *between* a moral presupposition (responsibility) and determinism which is a (possible) presupposition from another field (science).

It has, however, sometimes been held that a type of freedom/determinism issue can arise actually *within* morality – that the idea of moral responsibility, quite apart from its possible inconsistency with presuppositions from other fields, is *self*-contradictory. The line of thought is this: that for a person to be responsible for an action it must be *both* free (i.e. not causally determined) *and* yet done by him (i.e. caused by him or some motive in him and so causally determined). I think that there is little doubt that some moral philosophers have contrived to commit themselves to both of these incompatible propositions, but I also think that it is possible to give an adequate account of responsibility without doing so. The paradox of moral responsibility arises only

1. if freedom, in the morally relevant sense, is incompatible with causal determination, and
2. if what makes a person's action *his* is its being caused by him or by something in him.

Of these the former seems pretty clearly false – as Hume and many others have pointed out the opposite of 'free' (in the morally relevant sense) seems to be 'compelled' not 'caused'. And the second is at least doubtful. There is indeed a connection between a person's character, or motive, and his action, but it is more plausibly regarded as a logical than a causal connection. A generous character does not cause a man to perform generous actions, it is rather that by calling a man generous we *mean* that he is disposed to perform generous actions. And to say that an action is performed from a certain motive, is not to give a causal explanation of it but to describe it as being of a certain kind.

DUTY AND IGNORANCE

We may turn now to the second ground of exculpation: ignorance. Does it always exculpate? Examples so far given have been cases of ignorance of *fact*, not knowing that the gun was loaded, not knowing that someone was there. And this sort of ignorance indubitably does. The man who did not know the gun was loaded is not responsible, culpable, for killing the bystander. It does not necessarily follow, of course, that he is completely innocent – notoriously guns playfully pointed at people frequently are loaded – but what he is guilty of is gross carelessness with a fire-arm, not murder. He ought to have found out whether the weapon was loaded and he is culpable for not having done so. In cases where people's, humanly speaking, unavoidable factual ignorance or error leads to their performing actions which would be wrong if performed in full knowledge, we unhesitatingly find them guiltless. Nobody would blame a doctor for injuring a patient if all he had done was to assume that a drug from a reputable source was correctly labelled.

This notion of responsibility, which takes account of 'mental' factors, what the agent believes or intends as distinct from what is so or what results, is sometimes termed 'SUBJECTIVE RESPONSIBILITY' – not that it really needs a distinguishing epithet since it just is the notion of responsibility that we ordinarily employ. The point of the epithet is, however, to distinguish it from strict liability or OBJECTIVE RESPONSIBILITY, whereby a person is held to be responsible (guilty) provided only that he has 'performed' a wrong or forbidden action, quite irrespective of his state of mind. The English criminal law recognises certain offences of strict liability (e.g. under some pure food Acts and some traffic legislation), and Communist treason trials have sometimes condemned indisputably well-intentioned Party members for 'objectively' helping the class enemy when that has been deemed to be the (unintended) effect of their actions. It seems, however, to be one of the firmest characteristics of current morality that it has no room for objective responsibility. Oedipus was not *morally* responsible for killing his father and marrying his mother, both of which he did in ignorance. His horrible fate is not a vindication of, but an affront to, present-day morality. In this connection, it is interesting to notice that children appear for a time to employ a notion of objective responsibility before they develop the properly moral, subjective conception.

Corresponding to subjective and objective responsibility are the ideas of SUBJECTIVE and OBJECTIVE DUTY. The distinction can be illustrated in this way. A doctor needs to revive his patient. He gives an injection, but the ampoule through no fault of his is wrongly labelled and the man succumbs. The doctor clearly did what he thought he ought to do (i.e. his subjective duty) but, unhappily, because of error on a matter of fact, he did not do what really ought to have been done (i.e. his objective duty). Given this distinction, there then seems to arise the bizarrely baffling question: which ought one to do, one's objective or subjective duty? It is baffling because neither answer seems acceptable. It cannot be right to say that one ought to do what one merely thinks, very likely wrongly, ought to be done. But then neither does it seem correct to say, since 'ought' implies 'can' and we cannot always avoid mistakes, that one ought to do what really is right. The question is bizarre because it seems to suggest that an individual can somehow envisage, as alternatives between which he can choose, on the one hand what he thinks he ought to do and, on the other, what he really ought to do. The oddity and uncertainty are, however, the result of trying to ask too many questions at once, and they disappear once appropriate distinctions are made. We must first distinguish, from questions about the use of 'duty' and similar expressions, questions about responsibility or culpability to which we have already offered a partial answer. To the question about 'duty' – whether we should say a man had done his duty *only* if he had done what he really ought (the objective view) or whether we should allow that he had done his duty when he had only done what he (mistakenly) thought he ought (the subjective view) – no absolutely simple answer is possible. My own opinion (and this is simply a conjecture about current usage) is that we can safely say without qualification that a man has done his duty only when he has done what both he and we regard as really right. If we say that he has done his duty when, through innocent error of fact, he has done something that it would be wrong to do intentionally, we run the risk of being misunderstood unless we qualify our statement. But we are equally liable to be misunderstood if in such circumstances (where the assumption is that he is not *morally* culpable) we say that he has not done his duty. The objective view (considered as a view about the use of 'duty', *not* as a view about culpability) seems to me nearer to the truth, but it fails to do justice to the complexity of usage.

Perhaps it is not a specially interesting question to ask how the phrase 'he did his duty' is used. But the objective/subjective duty dispute is a good example of a philosophical problem which generates puzzlement because distinguishable questions (one about culpability, one about 'duty') are mixed up together. The dispute has usually been conducted in relation to the term 'duty', but it need not be so confined. Similar problems arise in connection with terms like 'obligation' and 'right'. Nor, though the disputants have usually been objectivists (i.e. have thought that there always is something that really is right or a duty as distinct from being *thought* to be so), does the dispute disappear if objectivism is abandoned. Whatever view be taken of the logical status of moral judgements, there will remain occasions on which people, on account of factual error, do things which both we and they agree it would be wrong to do in full knowledge. It would be an exaggeration to say that the view taken of moral judgements makes no difference to one's attitude to the dispute – it is bound to have a bearing on the relations between factual and moral error (ignorance) – but there is a problem concerning duty and ignorance on any view.

MORAL ERROR

So far the discussion of ignorance in relation to culpability and the application of the word 'duty' has taken account only of ignorance or error concerning matters of *fact*. But could there not also be *moral* ignorance and error? And, if so, what would be their impact on questions of culpability? Suppose, for instance, we think poorly of a young man for disappointing a girl's reasonable expectations. He might defend himself, not by arguing that he mistakenly thought that she understood the strictly short-term nature of his intentions, but by claiming that it is perfectly all right to secure a girl's co-operation by false protestations of undying love. Or suppose that someone claims that it is morally unobjectionable to steal from his employers or to falsify his income-tax returns. It is plain enough that many people, who in *our* view act wrongly, will claim with complete sincerity that in *their* view they are acting rightly, and in some cases the source of their wrongdoing (as *we* think it) will lie, not in errors of fact, but in 'errors', if that is the word, of moral judgement. True, the man who cheats the Inland Revenue may believe that it helps him and hurts no one else, and this may be false in fact, and it may even be that if we could persuade him that it was false, he would agree that he ought not to cheat. But there is surely no reason to suppose that this will always be so. It has to be allowed that people may be 'ignorant' or in 'error' (to put it no higher, that they may disagree with us) on matters of morality as distinct from matters of fact.

Factual error clearly exculpates. Does moral error do the same? Some certainly have thought so, and have reserved specifically *moral* condemnation for those who do what *they themselves* believe to be wrong. (Only 'subjectively' wrong action is necessarily morally culpable.) Full sincerity of moral conviction, that is to say CONSCIENTIOUSNESS in a common sense of the term, guarantees moral innocence, however wrong may be the conviction that is acted upon. This is by no means a comfortable conclusion – it obliges one to allow that Hitler, Stalin, or whoever one's favourite villain may be, might have been morally guiltless in that he might well have sincerely felt that what he did was right – but it is a position that some have thought unavoidable.

It may be made more palatable by insisting that villains normally are not sincere, despite their protestations they do really know that what they do is wrong (but can this, given our infinite capacity for self-deception, really be universally true?); or by taking a narrow view of *moral* condemnation which would permit one to hold that Hitler, for instance, though possibly not strictly speaking *morally* wicked, was nevertheless in some other sense a bad and dangerous man, whom it was a duty to oppose. This latter manoeuvre helps, but there is no doubt that many still jib at the idea that their villains may be in any sense morally innocent.

How can it be decided what is the correct view of moral error in relation to culpability? The 'moral consciousness', i.e. common opinion on moral matters, is here divided. On the one hand, immense importance and respect is accorded to sincerity and conscientiousness; on the other, there is resistance to the thought that really evil-doers can be sincere and conscientious. I have little doubt that waning confidence in accepted rules of *behaviour* tends to be compensated by an upgrading of conscientiousness and sincerity. When we are not sure what ought to be done, we are so much readier to entertain the idea that people may conscientiously differ. When we cannot agree what ought to be done, we can still perhaps agree that conscientious convictions should be respected. One not infrequently hears people talking as if they think that conscientiousness is the *only* thing that counts from the moral point of view, as if morally speaking it does not matter what people do so long as they sincerely think it right. But, while there may be room for disagreement about the relative emphasis to be placed on conduct and attitude (the act and agent aspects of morality, to employ a celebrated distinction of John Stuart Mill), it is absurd that conduct should count for nothing at all.

Views about the nature of moral judgements make a difference at this point. For some moral philosophers (objectivists, intuitionists – see chapter 5) moral judgements just are statements of some more or less special sort of fact. Since they are not different in principle from ordinary statements of empirical fact, it is only to be expected that moral errors would have the same bearing on issues of culpability as other factual errors. For other moral philosophers (subjectivists, emotivists, prescriptivists – see chapters 5 and 6), however, moral judgements are much more statements about or expressions of attitudes, decisions, imperatives, and on such views it is so unclear what is to be accounted moral error that it is by no means certain that it exculpates. Aristotle, interestingly, seems to have thought that moral, as opposed to factual, error does not exculpate ((1) Book 3). Indeed some contemporary prescriptivists, in this resembling Aristotle, find difficulty in allowing for the one sort of culpable conduct (i.e. doing what you are fully convinced is wrong) that the objective intuitionists typically recognise. If 'judging' something to be wrong is not so much making an assertion as deciding, committing oneself and enjoining others not to do it, then it is difficult to see how one can with full responsibility (voluntarily, deliberately) do what one with full conviction thinks wrong.

Acting contrary to sincere profession has for most moralists, from St Paul onwards, been a central feature of the moral life. But there have been others, from Plato to Hare, willing to deny or to make reservations about, its possibility. (They are sometimes said to embrace the 'SOCRATIC PARADOX'.) As usual, some of the disagreement on this issue derives from cross purposes and confusions. But mostly it reflects a fundamental divide in thought about conduct. In theoretical terms, it is between objectivists and their opponents. In practical terms there are on the one side those who have little doubt what is right (perhaps because they identify morality with some social code or the edicts of some church) and who consequently see the main moral problem as bringing oneself to do it, the only moral failure as not doing it. On the other side are those who see the main problem as one of discovering or deciding what ought to be done. In comparison the problem of getting oneself to do it seems quite trivial, and may be defined out of existence altogether. Positions in moral philosophy are determined partly by theoretical considerations, partly by interpretations of the presenting moral situation.

SUMMARY

Moral merit and demerit are not simply determined by the fulfilment or non-fulfilment of moral requirements, but by the idea of an average

D

level of fulfilment. It is also possible to earn merit by performing acts that go beyond duty. Puzzles, e.g. about acts of supererogation, derive from over-simplifications.

Exculpatory conditions can be collected under the heads of compulsion and ignorance. Physical compulsions are exculpatory. There are line-drawing problems with regard to threats and psychological compulsions. The determinism-based worry that nobody ever acts responsibly. 'Compelled' not 'caused' the opposite of 'free' in the sense relevant to moral responsibility.

Factual ignorance exculpates, although people may be to blame for not being properly informed. Moral responsibility is subjective rather than objective. Subjective and objective duty: it is necessary to distinguish questions about the use of 'duty' from questions about culpability.

Does moral 'error' exculpate in the same way as does factual error? Affirmative answer and associated view that conscientiousness guarantees moral innocence. This is further supported by objectivist analyses of moral judgements. On non-objectivist views it is unclear what moral error is and consequently uncertain whether it exculpates. The 'Socratic paradox', i.e. the refusal to concede without reservation that people may do what they think they ought not.

FURTHER READING

On acts of supererogation, there is an extensive recent periodical literature starting from Urmson (79). There are references in Carritt (10) and Raphael (56).

On responsibility, valuable discussions include Aristotle (1, Book 3); Hume (24, section 8); Ayer (3, chapter 12). Bradley (5) is interesting too. On psychological compulsions, especially with reference to legal conceptions of responsibility, see Wootton (73) and Hart (21). Hare (19, chapters 4 and 5) is relevant. For references on freewill and determinism see below, chapter 7, pages 103–6.

On duty and ignorance, see Prichard (53, chapter 2), also Carritt (10, chapter 2), Ross (59, chapter 7), Raphael (56, chapter 7), Baier (4, chapter 6), D'Arcy (12, chapter 3). On children employing an objective notion of responsibility, see Piaget (49).

On conscientiousness, see MacLagan (77), Nowell-Smith (44, chapters 17 and 18). Kant (29, section 1) is relevant. Mill's distinction between questions concerning the rightness of acts and those concerning the worth of agents is to be found in *Utilitarianism* (40, chapter 2). Since Hare (18, chapter 11.2), much has been written on acting contrary to profession, e.g. Gardiner (75), Ewing (13, chapter 1), Hare (19, chapter 5).

5 The Status of Moral Judgements – I

So far, we have been considering problems that arise *within* morality, partly by asking possibly slightly artificial questions, about such matters as conflicting duties and duties to oneself, which focus attention on points of special difficulty and importance. It has already appeared that some of these questions, notably those concerning moral error and action contrary to profession, cannot be answered without moving *outside* morality and raising more general, philosophical questions about the status of moral judgements. Up to now, in trying to answer the questions posed, we have in effect been drawing upon our acquaintance with moral concepts – we may not, of course, have had much practice in saying things about them, but we can hardly have failed to become accustomed to *using* them. Henceforward, the appeal will rather be to philosophical considerations of what does and does not make sense.

The status of moral judgements[1] and questions related to this have been the main topic of recent moral philosophy in English. Such an enquiry is obviously of great theoretical interest. A major philosophical concern has always been to give a comprehensive account of the main types of thing that can be significantly said, and moral judgements, since they at any rate *appear* to differ importantly from locutions belonging to other fields, clearly merit investigation from this point of view. But the examination of them is practically important too. Views about moral disagreement, toleration, moral education, the relative appropriateness of democratic and authoritarian systems of control and government, usually presuppose at least implicit conceptions of the status of moral judgements. Mill's celebrated defence of the 'liberty of thought and expression' (i.e. free speech), for instance, assumes that moral judgements are of the same status as the statements of science. If we doubt that, as we well may, but still want to defend free speech, we shall need to find supporting reasons different from those offered by Mill.

MORAL POSITIVISM

One possible, though not often explicitly maintained, view about moral judgements must be cleared aside before the point of the questions that will later be asked can become apparent. This is the view of morality as a code of informal legislation. General moral principles are held to be simply rules of conduct actually accepted in our society, and singular moral judgements to be just applications of these rules to particular cases.

On such a view, supposing it could be taken seriously, there would be no special problem about the status of moral judgements. They would be factual statements to the effect that such and such a rule was currently accepted, or that such and such an action conformed to one or other of the rules, and the practical force of moral judgements (as resolutions, injunctions to act) would derive from people's commitment to the current rules. Beyond this, all that would remain would be the possibility of explaining in psychological, sociological or historical terms why the current code is what it is.

Moral positivism is an outsider's view of morality, which is seen simply as a social code.

The inadequacies of the view begin to emerge as soon as one tries to assess the extent of the analogy between morality and law. There are very many differences: no moral legislatures, no courts of morals, no definite sanctions and no formal enforcement procedures. Because of this, while it is in principle a simple question of fact what the law on a given matter is (it is determined by what Parliament has enacted and/or the courts decided), there is no comparable way of finding out what is morally right or wrong. Of course, it is sometimes clear enough what some, most, or all people in a society think about some matter – but this is not to discover what *is* morally right or wrong, but only what is held to be so. If Parliament, by the proper procedure, has enacted a rule, if properly constituted courts have applied it, there is no question but that it is the law. Similarly, with custom and etiquette. If people mostly do certain things (like giving women precedence on social occasions) or object to others (like the omission of 'thank you' letters after visits), there is no doubting that they are customary or contrary to etiquette. In all these fields what *is* is, legally or as a matter of custom or etiquette, *right*. Not so with morality. Any number of people can hold something to be right without making it unchallengeably right. No matter what authority, church, government political party, popular newspaper (or even not so popular newspaper like *The Times* or *The Guardian*) pronounces something to be right, it still may intelligibly be questioned whether it is indeed morally right.

To this extent moral judgements seem to claim kinship with, among others, those of mathematics and natural science. They are to be accepted or rejected, not by reference to institutions and authorities, nor even to common opinion, but by standards belonging to their own conceptual field. The 'authorities' in such fields are those who are in the appropriate senses, wise, learned, or experienced, not simply those in a position to enforce their opinions or to be mouthpieces of majority views. It may be in the end with morality, as perhaps also with aesthetics and criticism, that the appearance is illusory – but it is at least plain enough to rule out the cruder sort of moral positivism.

MODELS FOR MORAL JUDGEMENTS

Moral judgements, it appears, are not simply factual statements about accepted codes (the *mores*). What sort of statements are they then – if indeed they are any sort of statements at all? It would obviously be very convenient if they turned out to be statements of some familiar and well-understood type. I do not myself think they will, but, nonetheless, views to the contrary deserve serious consideration. (Views according to which moral judgements express statements are often called COGNITIVIST. Views on which they are rather commands, wishes, expressions of attitude are accordingly NON-COGNITIVIST.)

Two sources of (possibly) well-understood types of statement are mathematics and empirical (natural or social) science. Morality has frequently been conceived on one or other of these models. If mathematics is the model, we may speak of ETHICAL RATION-ALISM, if science, of ETHICAL NATURALISM. Ethical rationalism and naturalism are then two species of cognitivism – though it must be recognised that all these terms are used in a variety of ways, and that 'naturalism' in particular is sometimes used with as wide a meaning as that assigned to 'cognitivism'.

I shall consider in turn how far moral judgements resemble the statements of mathematics or those of science, and then go on to consider the distinguishable, though related, question whether they are analytic or synthetic (empirical) statements.

ETHICAL RATIONALISM

This type of view, of which there have been numerous exponents from at least the seventeenth century to the present day, construes morality on a mathematical, specifically a geometrical, model. Euclidean geometry is a deductive system, consisting of *definitions* of such key terms as 'point', 'line' etc. and of *axioms*, for instance the axiom of parallels, which lays down that through a point outside a given straight line only one line can be drawn parallel to the given line. From the axioms are deduced *theorems*, such as that of Pythagoras, according to which the square on the hypotenuse of a right-angled triangle is equal to the sum of the squares on the other two sides. The theorems are true because they are deduced from the axioms, which must be true because they are SELF-EVIDENT. Or, as it may be said, the ground for accepting the theorems, is *demonstration*; the ground for accepting the axioms, *intuition*. Ethical rationalists are accordingly often called INTUITIONISTS, in as much as they hold that some moral principles have the logical status of geometrical axioms. Moral thinking is moreover like geometrical thinking in that it consists *either* in deriving subordinate moral principles ('theorems') from the ultimate ones ('axioms') *or* in applying a moral principle to a particular case. Concluding, in a particular case in which, say, a promise had been made that such and such ought to be done, would be like concluding that a particular figure must, by virtue of being a triangle, have its interior angles equal to two right angles.

Ethical rationalism fits in well with legalistic conceptions of morality. Moral agents apply the self-evident moral law much as the courts apply the law of the land. But, it may be asked, is this a correct account of the relationship in morality between general principles and judgements in particular cases? The assumption is that we have the general principles first and then simply deduce singular judgements from them. But are we really sure that, in reaching singular judgements to the effect, for instance, that such and such an action ought to be done, we are deducing what is already there in the general principles and not just making up our minds how to interpret the general principles or, indeed, just deciding what ought to be done in the particular case? Moral principles that have any claim to be self-evident are inevitably highly indeterminate, and it is certainly possible to feel surer of one's judgement in a particular case than of any reasonably precise moral principle it might be represented as being deducible from.

Considerations such as these, though they may raise doubts about the geometrical analogy, are not decisive. Historically, some geometrical truths were known before axioms had been formulated from which they could be deduced as theorems. It might, for all that has been said so far, still be the case that morality is awaiting its Euclid. But there are other, more serious difficulties for ethical rationalism.

One of these is the fact that moral principles, as commonly formulated, appear to be capable of conflicting. This is clearly inconsistent with any claim that they are, as formulated, self-evident, although, as we saw in chapter 2 there are various ways in which one may try to cope with conflicts of principles. Principles may be distinguished as those of perfect and imperfect obligation, some may be given precedence over others, or they may be interpreted as rules of *prima facie* as opposed to strict obligation. But, whatever the merits and demerits of particular manoeuvres, it must be said, first, that they all tend *both* to weaken the geometry/morality analogy *and* at the same time to diminish the attractions of ethical rationalism, which derive from its promising to supply axioms for *deciding* our moral perplexities.

The major objection to ethical rationalism is, however, that the central notion of self-evidence or intuition will not bear the weight placed upon it. We are not obliged to concede that there are any truths of substance, in morality, mathematics, or any-where else, that have to be accepted just because they appear self-evident. So long as it is believed that geometrical axioms are self-evident truths of substance, there is no objection *in principle* to the recognition of other self-evident truths in morality. But it no longer seems that the notion of self-evidence is needed in relation to mathematics – a point that can be more technically, though still not exactly, expressed by saying that mathematical statements are more plausibly held to be analytic than synthetic *a priori* (see pages 64–71). (Philosophy is one subject. Ethical rationalism fails as much because of developments in philosophy of mathematics as in moral philosophy itself.) For mathematics, there are in the ideas of analyticity and the postulates of a formal deductive system superior substitutes for the notion of self-evidence that are not available to morality. It is quite clear, as we shall see, that moral principles cannot be analytic.

I have been criticising ethical rationalism by drawing attention to deficiencies in the morality/mathematics analogy. But, it may be asked, is this analogy essential to the view criticised? It seems to me that content can be given to the obscure contention that the 'moral faculty' is reason in this sort of way, but there certainly have been ethical rationalists or intuitionists who did not stress the morality/mathematics analogy. One of them is Moore who argued, or asserted, in his *Principia Ethica* (43), that judgements to the effect that things are good in themselves attributed simple, 'non-natural', properties to their objects. The property denoted by the word 'good' in such judgements was, according to Moore, absolutely simple and quite different from any natural object, i.e. different from any *simple* property apparent to the senses such as redness, pleasantness, and from any *complex* property compounded out of simple ones which might belong to the subject matter of one of the natural or social sciences. Moore did not succeed, even to his own satisfaction, in making clear what he meant by a non-natural property, and the negative phraseology employed is surely significant. It is tempting to suppose that non-naturalism derives from the conviction that moral judgements *must*, if they are to be objective or even meaningful, attribute some sort of property to objects *together with* the recognition that they do *not* attribute natural properties. The difference between non-natural properties and non-properties is so fine as to have defied elucidation, and ethical non-naturalism seems to be little more than the denial of naturalism dressed up as a positive view. It is certainly arguable that the proper conclusion to be drawn from the rejection of naturalism is that moral judgements do not attribute any sort of properties to objects, that they are not indeed statements at all – and this is, in fact, the line of thought that leads to the non-cognitivistic views that will be considered in the next chapter. Nevertheless, it has to be recognised that the theses that moral judgements refer to properties of some sort, that they express statements of some sort, exhibit an extraordinary resistance to 'refutations'. So much so, that one is inclined to suppose that they will always have adherents in moral philosophy. Non-cognitivist views of one sort or another seemed to be gaining ground steadily for many years after 1945, but there are now signs that the high-water mark has been reached and the ebb set in.

ETHICAL NATURALISM

This, like the mathematically oriented species of ethical rationalism, denies that there is anything logically distinctive about moral judgements. It is sometimes felt that to take such views betrays a want of respect for morality, a tendency to explain it away or to reduce it to something else. Non-naturalists, who often also reject many sorts of rationalism, sometimes set themselves up as guardians of the uniqueness of morality, of the 'AUTONOMY OF ETHICS'. The trouble about uniqueness theses, however, is that they invariably admit of two interpretations, one strict and the other liberal; on the former of which they are all trivially true and on the latter as trivially false. There are inevitably some differences between moral judgements and other sorts of appraisal and assertion, but there are also similarities. It is not too difficult to pick out morality from other areas of concern, but it is certainly not the case that the *language* of morality is unique. The same basic vocabulary serves in all fields of evaluation. Much of what can be truly said of moral judgements would seem to apply to value judgements generally.

Naturalism construes moral judgements as statements of fact, on the model, it was said above, of the statements of science. This is, however, too narrow. Statements of fact also include everyday assertions about the weather, what one had for breakfast, and so forth. They range from, at one extreme, singular perception reports ('That object is blue') to, at the other, the highest-level statements of science (e.g. 'Bodies attract one another with a force proportional to their masses and inversely proportional to the square of the distance between them'). Naturalistic accounts of moral judgements exhibit the same range of variation.

There have, for instance, been '*moral sense*' views according to which statements that actions are right or things good are established by reference to the moral sense, in the way that statements about colours, textures, temperatures are established by sight, touch, feeling. There is some extravagance in the view, in that it is part of our concept of a sense that there should be some specific organ or set of nerve fibres for every sense. We may talk of moral sense, but we do not mean that we literally have a faculty of moral perception analogous to the sense of sight. There is, moreover, for moral sense views some difficulty in accounting for differences in moral opinion between people of different times and places. Of course, there are perceptual differences too, but these, unlike moral differences, do not tend to coincide with cultural boundaries, and such defects as blindness, colour-blindness, deafness, have physiological bases that are unavailable for their moral analogues. In its day, the moral sense theory was criticised for representing moral distinctions as arbitrary and subjective. The thought was that it implied that objects and actions were not good and right in themselves, but simply appeared to be so when they affected our moral sense. Our moral sense might have been different and, if it had been, we should have attributed different moral qualities to things, just as we should attribute different visual qualities (colours, etc.) to things if our eyes were different. Colours, in the eighteenth century, were widely thought of as 'secondary qualities', which were in the mind rather than in objects, and the moral sense theory was felt to imply that moral qualities were subjective in the same way. Nowadays, however, we are more likely to be impressed by objectivism than the subjectivism of a moral-sense view, mainly because we are likely to take a more realist (objectivist) view of the so-called secondary qualities, or at least to see no significant difference in point of objectivity between them and the so-called primary qualities of shape, size, mass, etc. This is yet another illustration of the way in which interpretations of ethical theories may be influenced by theories in other areas of philosophy.

Historically, the moral sense theory tended to develop into a still popular type of view according to which moral judgements make assertions about people's feelings or attitudes. Hume, for instance, claims that moral distinctions are derived from a moral sense, but what he means by this is that judging something morally good is asserting that it pleases one (perhaps in a special way) or that it evokes in one the pleasing sentiment of approbation. Such views are better called *moral sentiment* than moral-sense theories. It makes a difference what the moral sentiments are taken to be, and it is more plausible to regard moral judgements as reporting settled attitudes of approval and disapproval rather than occasional likings and dislikings, pleasures and pains. But for the present purpose it is necessary to consider moral sentiment views generally, and largely to neglect the many differences among them.

These views are SUBJECTIVIST when a moral judgement is taken to report the attitude of the *speaker*, i.e. when 'X is good' is taken to mean 'I approve of X'. When interpreted in this way, moral judgements are subjective on the two counts: that they say something about a person's feelings not about their ostensible object, and that there is at any rate no obvious sense in which they could be mistaken. A variant type of moral-sentiment view, according to which 'X is good' means 'X is approved of by all or most people' is subjectivist on the first count but not the second, for clearly a speaker can be mistaken about what all or most people approve, even though he can hardly be mistaken about what he approves himself.

The really puzzling question about moral-sentiment views is why, despite their manifest implausibility, they have such a widespread appeal. Indubitably, when people say that things are good they do, typically, have PRO-ATTITUDES towards them, but in saying that things are good they are not saying, or not *just* saying, that they have these attitudes. Retort to someone who says that something or other is good with 'You mean you like it (approve of it)' and he will not accept this as the equivalent of what he said, any more than a person will normally accept 'You mean you believe (are quite sure about) it' as a fair rendering of his claim to know it. 'Know' makes a claim that goes beyond an avowal of belief. 'Good' and other evaluative terms are used in ways which suggest that they too make claims that go beyond reports of attitudes. Why then is there such a tendency to interpret them as doing no more than make such reports? Part of the explanation is, I think, that there is a widespread and profound suspicion of moral judgements, a strong inclination to believe that moralists are prone to overrationalise what are substantially no more than arbitrary preferences, that they try to relieve feelings of insecurity by building up certain features of the use of the *word* 'good' into the thesis that moral judgements are objective. How far such suspicion is justified is a large question to which there is no easy answer. One relevant observation, though, is that if we turn to fields of evaluation other than the moral we find that there is often no great difficulty in distinguishing between saying that one has a pro-attitude towards something and saying that it is good. I may for instance like, enjoy, be prepared to recommend novels which by the appropriate standards (which include, for example, the requirement that characterisation should be psychologically realistic) are not good. Whenever standards can be in some degree specified in a field of evaluation, there is the possibility of distinguishing between reports of pro-attitudes and VALUE JUDGE-MENTS.

A problem for the type of subjectivist naturalistic account of moral judgements that we are considering is how to distinguish moral judgements in particular from other value judgements, which may of course be expressed in the same words. A common approach is to let the distinction depend on the nature of the feelings or attitudes expressed. Thus Hume, for instance, can be read as maintaining that all value judgements are reports to the effect that some object pleases, and that what makes a judgement moral is some peculiar quality of the pleasure in question. (He does not, alas, have much to say about wherein the peculiarity of moral pleasures consists.) The same line is often taken about aesthetic judgements. What makes them aesthetic is that they report attitudes of a particular aesthetic kind, which can be at any rate partially characterised as disinterested and contemplative rather than practical. It is in fact significantly difficult to give a *complete* characterisation of moral or aesthetic attitudes, and this raises a doubt about the soundness of the project of making the moral/aesthetic distinction in these terms (and hence about the subjectivist analysis of moral and aesthetic judgements). Should we in fact be prepared to deny that somebody was making a moral judgement just because his feelings or attitudes appeared not to be of the proper moral kind, whatever that may be? And, indeed, is there, in the end, any better way of characterising moral or aesthetic feeling or attitudes than (unhelpfully) as those we have when we make moral or aesthetic judgements?

We must now turn to the consideration of naturalistic views which are objectivist in that they represent moral judgements, not as psychological statements, but as statements about something other than feelings or states of mind. Examples of such views include evolutionist ethical theories, according to which such judgements as 'This practice (e.g. monogamy) is morally admirable' means (something like) 'This practice is found at a late stage in social evolution' or 'This practice tends to promote the survival of the social group'. Utilitarianism, considered as a theory about the meaning of moral terms or the analysis of moral judgements, also comes into this category. Bentham, for instance, sometimes writes as if he thought that 'You ought to do X (e.g. repay the money you borrowed)' meant 'Doing X will produce more happiness (or less unhappiness) for everybody it affects than any other action open to the agent in the circumstances'. It is, of course, doubtful whether these views and others of their type do what they set out to do, and re-express moral judgements as strictly natural (i.e. factual) statements. Certainly the allegedly factual statements produced are normally extremely vague and/or or ambiguous, and moreover hardly possible of verification. There are, too, special difficulties for each specific type of naturalistic view, evolutionist, utilitarian, or whatever it may be. But more interesting for the purpose of this book is the suggestion, frequently made since Moore's *Principia Ethica* of 1903, that *all* such views are incorrect because they commit the same NATURALISTIC FALLACY. This is supposed to be brought out by the alleged fact that, *however* a practice or action is characterised as highly evolved, tending to maximise happiness, etc., it will always be significant to ask whether (possible without contradiction to deny that) the practice so characterised is morally good. This shows that 'morally good' cannot be analysed in the ways suggested. Because a triangle can be defined as a three-sided figure, it does not make sense to ask whether (is contradictory to deny that) a triangle is a three-sided figure. The question is senseless and the denial contradictory in the way it is senseless to ask whether (is contradictory to deny that) a rose is a rose or a haystack a haystack.

Can it really be allowed that there is here an effective refutation (which could be called Moore's 'open question' argument) against *all* forms of ethical naturalism – if it works at all it will work against subjectivist as well as objectivist views? The thesis that there is has been hailed as the most important achievement of theoretical ethics. But we must not be misled by the rather obvious inadequacies of the very few naturalist views we have considered into overestimating the force of the open question argument or the genuineness of the fallacy it is supposed to expose.

What does the argument prove? Suppose that we seem to be able significantly to ask the question of every definition of 'good' and other evaluative terms. Suppose, that is, that whenever a evaluative term 'V' is defined naturalistically as '$A.B.C.$' it makes sense to ask whether something which is $A.B.C.$ is V. It does not strictly *follow* that the evaluative term in question is radically different from any naturalistic (factual) term. It may simply be that the evaluative term is vague and/or ambiguous. Additionally, it is not enough that it should be possible to ask the question in the sense that it 'sounds all right' (i.e. is not *linguistically* odd) to do so, for it will always sound all right if the defining phrase is verbally different from the words defined. What is required is that the question should be logically open in the way it is in relation to an inadequate definition and is not in relation to a correct one, but there is no way of determining this *independently* of determining the correctness or otherwise of the definition. The open question argument is, alas, like so many simple, general arguments in philosophy, either inadequate or superfluous.

My own opinion is that there is a naturalistic fallacy, i.e. that ethical naturalism is *in principle* unacceptable, although I do not know how this view can be conclusively established. It is, however, a good deal more certain that all naturalistic views so far produced are defective. The charms of ethical naturalism are very great. If it could be accepted, moral judgements could be established in the same sort of way, and with the same sort of cogency, as the statements of natural and social science. Philosophers often slide into naturalism because they are faced with the need to support some substantial moral principle. They begin by holding that, for instance, the greatest happiness of the greatest number is the one end at which we ought to aim (utilitarianism). Understandably, the principle is questioned, so they seek to defend it by claiming that it follows from the meaning of 'ought'. To say that one ought to do something is simply to say that it tends to promote the greatest happiness of the greatest number. Now, if there is a naturalistic fallacy, it has already been committed. 'Ought', being a value word, could not have such an (intentionally) purely factual meaning. But even if it could, too high a price would have been paid to support the utilitarian principle. It begins as a substantial, and therefore non-analytic, moral principle. It ends as analytic, and, therefore, lacking in moral substance. Why this is so we shall see in the next section. A naturalist may be perfectly consistent, and if he is, it is by no means certain that he can be refuted. But most naturalists are inconsistent in that they tend to hold that some moral principle is *both* analytic (i.e. when it needs justifying) *and* non-analytic (i.e. when it is to be used as a guide to conduct).

ANALYTIC AND SYNTHETIC STATEMENTS

The word 'analytic' has already been employed on one or two occasions. It has, for instance, been suggested that analyticity bears some relationship to self-evidence, and that no moral judgement can be analytic. It is now time to give a more explicit account of the meaning of ANALYTIC and of that of its opposite SYNTHETIC. These terms were introduced into philosophy by Kant in order to mark a distinction between two types of judgement or statement – a distinction which had been half recognised by some of his predecessors (notably Hume) but of which Kant was the first to form a reasonably clear conception. Examples of analytic statements include 'A square has four sides' and 'Material things occupy space'. Synthetic statements include 'The cheapest four-seater car costs about £500' and 'The eastern side of England is the colder and dryer'. Each of these statements may be said to have a logical subject, about which something is said in the rest of the statement, i.e. the predicate. They are all examples of sub-ject-predicate statements. The aptness of the terms 'analytic' and 'synthetic' emerges if one reflects that the relationship between subject and predicate is different in the first pair of statements from the second. A square is by definition a four-sided figure. By *analysing* the subject concept, squareness, one can see that it contains the predicate concept, four-sidedness. Similarly, with material things and occupying space. It is perhaps not clear what would be a full definition of the concept material thing, but occupying space is certainly part of it. Statements in which subject and predicate are related in the way described are called analytic. In the latter pair of statements, however, the relation is different. That costing £500 is not part of the concept, cheapest four-seater car, is evident from the fact that in 1939 the cheapest four-seater cost only £100. The case is the same with the eastern side of England and its weather. It could, because of major climatic changes, cease to be the drier and colder side – but nothing could conceivably stop a square being a four-sided figure. Non-analytic statements are called synthetic. Their predicate concepts are not contained in their subject concepts but, as it were, added to or synthesised with them.

It may be said, a little imprecisely, that analytic statements are true by definition whereas synthetic ones are not. Certainly, anyone who fails to accept the simple sort of analytic statement so far illustrated betrays a want of understanding of one or other of the words involved. In addition to statements true by definition, there are also statements false by definition. For instance, 'This circle is square' or 'This invisible gas can be seen'. It would be convenient to speak of analytically-true and analytically-false statements, but it is in fact more usual to call statements that are false by definition contradictions. To negate an analytic statement produces a contradiction, e.g. 'A square has *not* got four sides', and to negate a contradiction produces an analytic statement, e.g. since 'This circle is square' is a contradiction, 'This circle is *not* square' is analytic. Synthetic statements, on the other hand, even if true, may be negated without contradiction; and when they are false they may be negated without producing an analytic statement. Thus, 'The Serpentine froze in July 1968' is a false synthetic statement. Negating it produces a true synthetic statement, not an analytic one.

It is now possible to characterise an analytic statement as one of which the negation is contradiction, and a synthetic statement as one of which this is not the case. This is an improvement on characterising analytic statements as ones of which the predicate concept is contained in the subject concept, because a number of statements which should be classed as analytic are not of the subject-predicate form at all. To negate, for instance, 'If A is taller than B, and B is taller than C, then A is taller than C' yields a contradiction, but one cannot sensibly distinguish subject and predicate in this relational statement.

There are some further features of analytic and synthetic statements of which note should be taken. Analytic statements are *explicative*, they make plain the content and relations of concepts but they do not convey substantial (extra-conceptual) information to anyone who already understands the words in which they are expressed. It is not exactly news that a square has four sides, or even that a dodecagon has twelve. But it might be news, even to someone who understood the statement perfectly well, that the cheapest four-seater car costs something in the region of

E

£500. Synthetic statements are, therefore, *ampliative* as opposed to explicative. They may add to our knowledge of fact.

Connected with the explicative/ampliative difference is another difference between analytic and synthetic statements. The truth of the former can be established by purely logical or linguistic procedures, while that of the latter cannot. There is no need to refer beyond an analytic statement, to compare it with reality or the facts, in order to see that it is true. It is enough to attend to the meaning of the words with which it is expressed. Not so with synthetic statements. Whether they are true or false is not determined by their meaning, but depends on their relation to something else. In order to find out whether they are true or false, one has accordingly to pay attention to that something else, to make observations or conduct experiments. Because the truth or falsity of synthetic statements depends on something outside them, they are CONTINGENT (non-necessary). Since the truth of analytic statements is determined by the nature of the statements themselves, they are NECESSARY. It is because analytic statements are merely explicative (not information imparting to those who understand them) that they are necessary: and because synthetic statements are ampliative that they cannot be necessary. An incapacity to convey extra-conceptual information is the price of necessity.

It is one of the defects of the idea of self-evidence, which was considered in connection with ethical rationalism above, that it obscures this point. It is natural, if self-evidence is to be placed by reference to the analytic/synthetic distinction, to align it with analyticity. But then self-evident statements would have to be merely explicative – a consequence disappointing to rationalists, whose object in employing the idea of self-evidence is to represent some statements (moral judgements or principles) as both necessary (undeniable) and yet at the same time not empty in the way that analytic statements are. The attractiveness of self-evidence vanishes once the analytic/synthetic distinction is made. Self-evidence, if it is not taken to be the equivalent of analyticity, tends to degenerate into the highly subjective notion of obviousness (but see pages 71–3).

The emphasis placed on the emptiness of analytic statements

may suggest that they are unimportant or pointless. This is far from being so, although misunderstandings of this nature are not uncommon in the history of philosophy, and a number of writers have dismissed analytic statements as trivial or merely verbal. But analytic statements express relations between concepts, between the meanings of words. Definitions generate analytic statements: it is because 'triangle' is defined as 'three-sided figure' that 'Triangles are three-sided' is analytic. Moreover, analyticity and the related notion of contradictoriness are connected with the idea of a *valid deductive argument*. When an argument is deductively valid, the conjoint assertion of the premises with the *negation* of conclusion will be contradictory, and the implication statement formed by putting 'if' before the premises and 'then' between them and the conclusion will be analytic. A set of analytic statements may, in effect, record a set of valid argument forms.

This helps to explain how it can be held that the obviously important statements of mathematics are analytic. The rather informal notion of analyticity so far set up hardly does justice to the nature of mathematical statements, but it does seem that they share with analytic statements both necessity and informational emptiness. It is superfluous to make observations or conduct experiments in order to establish that $2 + 2 = 4$ or that the sum of the interior angles of a triangle is two right angles. Nor could observation or experiment give any reason for doubting such statements – if observations run counter to them, we simply conclude that we have misobserved. Mathematical formulae can, however, be regarded as records of valid argument forms, in accordance with which it may be concluded, for instance, that *if* here are two pennies and there are two pennies *then* (subject to certain conditions) there will be four pennies altogether. Mathematics does not contain (empirical) information but, like logic and analytic truths generally, is of use in the processing of it.

It will by now be apparent that the question raised above whether moral judgements are more like the statements of mathematics (ethical rationalism) or more like those of natural and social science (ethical naturalism), can be re-formulated as the question whether they are analytic or synthetic (empirical) statements. It has already been suggested that there are reasons for rejecting both rationalism and naturalism. We must now see what form these conclusions take when related to our new question.

Are moral judgements analytic? It certainly appears that analytic statements can be constructed out of moral terms. For instance: 'Murder (presumably to be defined as "wrongful killing") is wrong' or 'One ought to do one's duty (where "duty" is defined as "what one ought to do")'. But on reflection it can be seen that these, indubitably necessary, moral 'judgements' have the sort of emptiness which characterises analytic statements generally and which is not a feature of moral judgements proper. The non-analytic 'Thou shalt not kill' has some moral substance about it. It tells one not to perform a certain sort of act. 'Murder is wrong', interpreted as analytic, does not tell one not to do anything specific. It tells one only that, *if* something is classified as murder, then it ought not to be done. But it does not tell one what cases of killing are to be accounted murders. Analytic statements constructed out of moral terms seem to be as distinct from moral judgements proper as analytic statements constructed out of factual terms (e.g. 'If it is invisible it is colourless') are distinct from (non-analytic) factual statements proper (e.g. 'It is invisible' or 'It is coloured').

Are moral judgements synthetic (empirical) statements? Do we, can we, establish by observation, experiment, etc. that people are good, actions right, or such that they ought to be done? I think that the answer is No, but the question is by no means a simple one. Obviously we cannot see, or otherwise observe, that a person is good in the way that we can see that an apple is red. Moral judgements do not attribute simple, perceptual qualities to their objects – nor is there, we have already decided, a special moral sense. But then very many synthetic empirical statements do not do so either. It cannot be seen, or otherwise directly observed, that a person is intelligent or businesslike. In investigating the truth of many factual statements, complicated tests and enquiries may be necessary, and appeal often has to be made to standards (of intelligence, or businesslikeness, etc.) which are not in any obvious way dictated by the nature of what the statements are about.

Moral judgements plainly differ from some synthetic (empirical) statements, but to show that they differ from them all would involve the consideration of an enormous range of examples. There is no really satisfactory alternative to a policy of thoroughness – philosophical conclusions are too often hastily drawn on the basis of a cursory consideration of a few, possibly atypical, examples – but, with misgivings, we must for the present purpose try to find a short cut to a significant difference between synthetic (empirical) statements and moral judgements. (One would like to find a crucial example, but in philosophy experience shows that every example can be reconciled with any theory.) Suppose we contrast disagreement over whether a car is economical with disagreement over whether one is good. In both cases the disputants will have to examine the car and put it through its paces (i.e. to make observations) and this may suffice to settle either matter for them, though in either case it may not. If disagreement persists after all relevant observations have been made, then the residual issue must concern standards, i.e. what is to be counted as economical or good. I incline to hold that the difference between factual and evaluative matters comes out in the following way: that there is a sense in which dispute about standards of economy is purely verbal, whereas dispute about standards of goodness is not. People may simply agree to differ on a verbal issue. Granted that the car is economical by one standard and not by another, there is no non-linguistic question left to be asked by the formula 'But is it *really* economical?', although it does, of course, remain an open question which sort of economy is to be preferred. When, however, a vehicle is good by one standard but not by another, there does seem to be a question left to be asked by the formula 'Is it *really* good?' That is, the question which standard is the right one, a question to which the answer has a close bearing upon the question which car is to be preferred. It is an entirely open question whether we ought to prefer a car which is in any sense economical, but it is not an open question whether we ought to prefer a car which we concede to be good.

If so much is granted (and it would be a great deal), the next question is whether the same relation as holds between economy and goodness in cars holds between (factual) questions whether a person is, say, businesslike and (moral) questions whether he is good. I do myself think that this is so; that disputes about standards of businesslikeness are verbal in the sense that they turn on what we choose to mean by 'businesslike', while disputes about moral standards are substantial; that, to put it another way, choice of moral standards matters more (makes more difference) than does choice of standards of businesslikeness. Our practical, not merely linguistic choices and preferences are reflected in the moral standards we adopt, which is why these standards, and judgements based on them, are authoritative for us. It follows that there may be irreducible differences over evaluative and moral issues – a conclusion which, however discouraging from a practical point of view, surely ought not be *philosophically* unwelcome, for we plainly do encounter irreconcilable differences in such matters.

I am contending that the significant difference between the fields of morality and value generally on the one hand and fact on the other is that there is scope for choice of standards in the former in a sense in which there is not in the latter. I am very conscious that I have done little towards establishing this. Clearly, any reason that could be found for holding that moral and evaluative standards are dictated by the nature of the objects evaluated would be a point on the other side. And it is arguable that standards for evaluating certain things – those made to perform definite purposes, like tools, instruments, machines, etc. – are fixed. Screwdrivers, it may be felt, have to be judged good or bad according by whether they drive screws well or ill; watches according to the quality of their time-keeping, and so on. I personally doubt whether we are *forced* to take this view even of the evaluation of tools – we surely need not evaluate them by functional standards, though we usually do – but we can concede so much without compromising our view of moral judgements. For of their objects, people are not made for any particular purpose, though they have purposes; and actions, though they are often performed for some purpose are not, from the moral as opposed to the prudential point of view, judged good or bad according to whether they do or do not serve the agent's purposes. We certainly do, and conceivably must, evaluate some things functionally: but we do not do so when we evaluate morally.

All this is on the assumption that there can be no purpose for people distinct from the purposes individual persons may have. But, of course, on some religious views people would be made for a purpose not their own. For the upholder of such view it would be natural to assimilate moral evaluation much more closely to the evaluation of objects like tools and instruments. No field of philosophical enquiry can be finally separated from any other, and here as elsewhere the view one takes in ethics will be quite reasonably influenced by one's view in another field.

THE SYNTHETIC A PRIORI AND THE VERIFICATION PRINCIPLE

It has been contended that moral judgements are neither analytic nor synthetic empirical statements, whence, since it is not clear that there are any other sorts of statements, it would seem to follow that they cannot be statements at all. But, it may be asked, is not this an absolutely disastrous conclusion for morality? If moral judgements are not even statements, must they not be held to be meaningless or nonsensical?

This very radical conclusion was in fact drawn by some of the philosophers (logical positivists) who accepted the so-called verification principle in the 1930s. The VERIFICATION PRIN-CIPLE stipulates in effect that to be significant or meaningful a statement must be analytic or empirical – no third possibility being allowed. There is no doubt that acceptance of the verification principle stimulated attempts to find satisfactory interpretations of moral judgements according to which they were not statements, and, therefore, not nonsensical, meaningless or pseudo-statements, although later on such non-cognitivist analyses of moral judgements came to seem eligible in their own right. Non-cognitivism in ethics survives in circles where the verification principle is no longer in vogue. (It should be noted that the verification principle *by itself* does not require the adoption of a non-cognitivist view. What does require such a view is the verification principle *plus* the conviction that moral judgements are not either analytic or synthetic empirical statements.)

In the event the verification principle has been very largely abandoned. It is not a true (synthetic empirical) report of the kinds of statements normally held to be meaningful. And, if it is claimed to be analytic it could be so only in virtue of a stipulative (non-standard) definition of meaningfulness, which there is no reason to adopt. It is thus not at all clear that the verification principle has any authority, and moreover there are very great difficulties in devising a satisfactory formulation of it. The hope was that it would make a clear distinction between sense and nonsense, but if formulated strictly enough to exclude all manifest nonsense it excludes a certain amount of obvious sense, and *vice versa*. It seems impossible to get it exactly right, and the moral most usually drawn is that the quest for a simple, general criterion of meaningfulness is misguided in principle.

If the verification principle is given up, could there not then be a third type of statement, which was neither analytic nor synthetic empirical? There can not indeed be statements that are neither analytic nor synthetic, that distinction is dichotomous, i.e. exclusive and exhaustive, but the nature of the analytic/synthetic distinction is not such that every synthetic statement has to be empirical. The empirical/non-empirical, or A POSTERIORI/A PRIORI distinction, the distinction between statements which can only be established empirically (by observation, experiment, etc.) and those which do not need to be established in this way, is independent of the analytic/synthetic distinction. In terms of the two distinctions, all analytic statements must be non-empirical (*a priori*), and all empirical statements must be synthetic, but there could be statements which are both synthetic and *a priori*. Kant, for instance, thought examples of such statements were to be found in mathematics (e.g. 'Two straight lines cannot enclose a space'), and in natural science (e.g. 'Every event has a cause'), and that making sense of them was a very difficult problem which he could nevertheless solve. Ethical rationalists, with their sometimes rather confused idea that moral judgements may be self-evident without being analytic, are in effect holding them to be synthetic *a priori*.

It is, however, very doubtful whether synthetic *a priori* statements have the philosophical importance claimed for them by Kant. They are not, for instance, a homogeneous category of statement. 'Synthetic *a priori*' sounds like a positive characterisation, but in fact it is equivalent to '*non*-analytic, *non*-empirical'. All that there is here is a set of very disparate problem statements, not a single type of statement. It is moreover significant that Kant took a very narrow view of analyticity, and therefore counted as synthetic *a priori* the statements of mathematics, which it would be more natural to regard as analytic. If it had to be conceded that indisputable examples of synthetic *a priori* statements were to be found in mathematics, or elsewhere, then one could more readily contemplate the possibility of there being further examples in morality. But as it does not, the case for this type of ethical rationalism cannot be made out.

SUMMARY

The present chapter, unlike previous ones which were mainly concerned with questions arising within morality, raises questions about morality, notably about the status of moral judgements.

If morality is viewed simply as a social code (moral positivism), there is no special problem about moral judgements. It seems that with regard to morality, as distinct from custom and etiquette, a distinction has to be drawn between what *is held to be* and what *is* right.

Moral judgements are sometimes construed on the model of mathematical statements (ethical rationalism) or the statements of empirical science (naturalism).

Ethical rationalism: moral principles and judgements are taken to resemble geometrical axioms and theorems. But are we more certain of moral principles than of moral judgements in particular cases? Conflict of moral principles as a difficulty for rationalism. Deficiencies of the notions of self-evidence and intuition (see also last section). Ethical rationalism without the mathematical analogy.

Ethical naturalism: moral judgements as statements of fact. Moral sense views – but there is not literally a moral *sense*. The view that moral judgements report feelings or attitudes. The sense in which such views are subjectivist and why they appeal. What according to views of these types distinguishes moral from, for example, aesthetic judgements. Objectivist naturalistic views, e.g. evolutionist theories and utilitarianism. The naturalistic fallacy and the possibility of refuting naturalism. Inconsistent naturalism.

The distinction between analytic and synthetic statements. The necessary, but merely explicative, nature of the former; the ampliative, but non-necessary, nature of the latter. The importance of analytic statements, and the extent to which mathematical statements resemble analytic ones.

Analytic statements can be constructed out of moral terms, but moral judgements proper are not analytic. Nor do they seem to be synthetic empirical statements – but the full range of such statements is not surveyed. It is suggested that the essential difference between the fields of fact and morality is that choices and preferences are reflected in moral standards. For this reason, there can be irreducible substantial differences in morality.

Moral evaluation is not functional, except possibly on some religious views.

The verification principle stipulates that there can be no statements that are neither analytic nor empirical. But if the verification principle is rejected, there could be a third category of synthetic *a priori* statements to which moral judgements might belong. It is, however, suggested that there is in fact no such homogeneous category of statement, and consequently no case for allocating moral judgements to it.

NOTES

1. *Moral judgements.* I employ this phrase, in accordance with widespread philosophical usage, to refer to characteristically moral locutions to the effect that an action is (morally) right or wrong, or such that it (morally) ought or ought not to be done, or that a person is (morally) good or bad, and so on. Moral judgements are commonly contrasted with factual statements and compared with value judgements from other fields, e.g. aesthetics. The employment of the term 'judgement' is in line with this. It would seem question begging to call them moral *statements*, since the contrast between moral judgements and factual statements is often expressed by saying that the former are not statements at all. If they are called judgements, it is an open question whether or not moral judgements are a species of statement.

This use of the term 'judgement' is, however, somewhat different from a common use in ordinary speech. There, the term is frequently employed in connection with the idea of using one's judgement as, for instance, in estimating distances as opposed to measuring them. Judging, in this sense, occurs in the realm of fact.

Anyone who fails to distinguish this sense of 'judgement' from the sense in which the term bears in the phrase 'moral judgement', may be led to believe that those who make a factual statement/moral judgement distinction are denying that judging (= estimating) takes place in relation to factual questions. This, of course, would be an absurd view. Alternatively, they may be led to conclude from the very obvious fact that judging (= estimating) does go on in the factual field that there is no distinction between factual statements and moral judgements. This is not an absurd conclusion, but it should not be accepted simply because of a confusion between two senses of 'judgement'.

I have some misgivings about the effectiveness of the sort of explanation I have given in rendering the phrase 'moral judgement', and indeed 'value judgement' too, unmisleading. It might be better to employ some artificial and therefore innocuous term such as 'locution'. One could then speak quite non-committally of factual, moral, value, etc. locutions. On balance, however, it seemed worth taking the risks involved in continuing with the more usual 'judgement'.

FURTHER READING

For the classic defence of the liberty of thought and discussion, see Mill *Liberty* (40). There is some discussion of alternative philosophical bases for this defence in Whiteley (71, chapter 7) and Mitchell (42, chapter 6).

For differences between morality and law, see Hart (20, chapter 8), for morality and custom Baier (4, chapters 1 and 5). For a statement of a very sophisticated form of moral positivism, see Lamont (33).

Ross (58, 59) and Prichard (53) are rationalist writers who emphasise the analogy between morality and mathematics. Price (52) is an earlier writer strikingly similar to Ross. Moore (43) is a rationalist who does not stress the analogy.

For the description and criticism of naturalism, see Moore (43). There are valuable discussions of him in Schilpp (60). There is an extended discussion of the naturalistic fallacy in Prior (54). See also Frankena in Foot (82). It obtains some consideration at least in nearly all recent general works on ethics.

For moral sense views, see Hutcheson (26), for comment Raphael (55). For moral sentiment views, see Hume (25). For evolutionist views, Spencer (64) is the classic source, and Huxley (27) and Waddington (70) are recent exponents. For a recent critical discussion, see Flew (14). Objectivist and subjectivist naturalistic views are, rather briskly, 'refuted' in Ayer (2, chapter 6).

The analytic/synthetic distinction is to be found in Kant (28, Introduction). For a balanced expression of current opinion, see

Hospers (23) who also gives an account of current views on mathematics. The only contemporary writer I know who actually regards moral judgements as analytic is Kaufmann (31, chapter 9) – the view is heavily qualified, however. After a long period of decline naturalistic views are again being defended, e.g. by Foot and Geach (in 82), who take the functionalist line. There is a discussion of functional words in relation to evaluation in Hare (18).

Ayer (2) is the best source for a defence of the verification principle. For contemporary opinion see Hospers (23), also for a discussion of the synthetic *a priori*.

6 The Status of Moral Judgements – II

NON-COGNITIVISM

Ethical rationalism feeds on the difficulties of ethical naturalism, naturalism on those of rationalism. The case for either is largely a set of objections to the other. If, therefore, neither kind of cognitivism is acceptable, there is a case for seeking a third alternative. Rationalism and naturalism, depite the opposition between them, perhaps make the same fundamental mistake of supposing that moral judgements must be statements. Concede that they need not be and a new prospect of making progress in moral philosophy opens up.

NON-COGNITIVISM inherits some of the appealing features of both rationalism and naturalism. The rationalist is anxious to deny that moral judgements are ordinary (naturalistic) statements of fact, that terms like 'right' and 'good' denote merely natural properties, and the non-cognitivist agrees with him, though for different reasons. On the other side, the naturalist wants to deny that moral judgements have any reference to such occult entities as non-natural properties, and the non-cognitivist agrees with that, too. A major consideration favouring rationalism in ethics in this century has been the desire to maintain the 'autonomy of ethics', to resist its 'reduction' to science or matters of fact, and non-cognitivist views can be interpreted as fulfilling this requirement in the most emphatic way possible. If moral judgements are not *statements*, they manifestly cannot be *factual* statements. From the non-cognitivist point of view there is the widest possible logical gulf between fact and value. For anyone who thinks there is indeed a great gulf here, non-cognitivism has the merit of offering an explanation of it.

Overt, self-conscious non-cognitivism is a twentieth-century phenomenon, but some earlier ethical theories lend themselves to reinterpretation in these terms. Hume, for instance, denied that moral judgements expressed either relations of ideas or matters of fact (i.e. roughly, that they were either analytic or synthetic statements), but proceeded nonetheless inconsistently to represent them as statements about people's feelings, that is, as matters of psychological fact. He would have done better to deny that they were statements at all. Kant, too, in making morality a matter of practical as opposed to theoretical reason, of the will rather than the understanding, can be helpfully interpreted on non-cognitivist lines.

Non-cognitivism in ethics had all the marks of a philosophical breakthrough, the way out of an impasse, a starting point for new enquiries, a key to much that had seemed obscure in the history of the subject. By now, however, these high hopes are beginning to fade. Revolutions, in philosophy as elsewhere, do not change things out of all recognition. Each bright, new dawn soon fades into common day.

THE EMOTIVE THEORY

This is the view that moral judgements are not statements about but expressions of feelings or attitudes. To say that something is, for instance, good is not to say that one approves of it, but to express or give vent to one's approval; to say that something is bad is to express one's disapproval or distaste. Moral judgements express feelings in the way that interjections and exclamations – 'Hurrah!', 'Boo', 'Splendid', 'Oh dear', etc. – express them; they are less like statements than cries of joy or pain.

In the case of its best known English exponent, Ayer, the emotive theory is the offspring of a marriage between the verification principle and the rejection of ethical naturalism. Or it can be regarded as a form of subjectivism revised to avoid committing the naturalistic fallacy. It seems that 'X is good' cannot be rendered as 'I approve of X' (conceived as a statement about my feelings); let it then be regarded simply as a linguistic means of expressing those feelings. The crucial question for emotivism is, therefore, whether the distinction between expressing feelings and saying that one has them will take the strain imposed upon it. That there is the possibility of such a distinction is apparent from the fact that one can express emotions without saying that one has them, as when, for instance, a person makes a remark about some such neutral subject as the weather in a voice trembling with anger, or utters what is in itself a harmless observation in a tone of loathing or contempt. It is a little more difficult to state that one has feelings without at the same time expressing them, for if the statement is seriously asserted (i.e. not simply entertained as an example of an autobiographical statement) the speaker is necessarily declaring that he has the feelings in question. It is possible, though significantly strange, to conceive of someone saying that he is very angry in a tepid, neutral tone; but there is a sort of pragmatic contradiction in temperately observing that one is beside oneself with rage.

Examples such as these may help to illustrate the expressing/ stating distinction, but it is doubtful whether they give the emotivist all he needs. He maintains that the words 'good', 'right', 'ought', etc., at least when used in their specifically ethical senses, somehow succeed in expressing feelings without saying that the the speaker has them. There are words in the language – 'ugh', 'pshaw', 'ouch' and so forth – of which this might be said, though even this is doubtful since there are occasions on which uttering one of these words is tantamount to making a statement. A man who denied that he had stated that it hurt him, on the grounds that all he said was 'ouch', which is not a statement, would certainly be guilty of disingenuousness. The most it seems possible to maintain with confidence is that, *if* there are any words that are purely emotive, they must be akin to the interjections and exclamations we have considered. It seems, then, that the emotivist is committed to maintaining that sentences containing 'good', 'right', 'ought' etc. are, from the logical or philosophical, if not grammatical, point of view, to be counted as interjections. This is not very plausible, if only because moral locutions at least *appear* to be capable of standing in logical relations to one another while interjections do not. One can, it seems, deny moral judgements, argue from them as premises to other moral judgements, find inconsistencies between them – none of which is possible with interjections.

It is no necessary part of the emotivist's intention (logically speaking) to downgrade moral judgements to the level of interjections, but this is the price of getting them on to the expressing side of the expressing/stating divide, which emotivists must do if their view is not to collapse into the subjectivism they reject. It is also doubtful whether modified forms of emotivism, according to which moral judgements have *both* DESCRIPTIVE *and* EMOTIVE MEANING (i.e. make statements about feelings or attitudes and also express them), escape the charge of naturalism. They are better regarded as sophisticated and subtle versions of naturalism, in which due account is taken of the non-cognitive aspects of moral judgements. If the judgement on naturalism expressed in the previous chapter is correct, such views are mistaken in principle, but at least one writer, Stevenson, has nevertheless used them as vehicles for expressing many valuable insights into the role of moral and other value judgements in discourse. In philosophy, it is in some ways less important to be right than to be thorough and acute.

One thing emotivists were able to do was to offer an alternative explanation of a feature of moral judgements which has frequently been thought to demand a cognitivist and indeed objectivist analysis of them. 'This is red' and 'This is not red', said of the same object at the same time, are contradictories of which one must be true and the other false. Similarly, 'This is good' and 'This is not good' at least *appear* to be contradictories, from which it would follow that they must be statements (only statements can be true or false), and statements about something other than the speaker's feelings or attitude. For there is no contradiction between, for example, 'I approve of X' and 'I do not approve of X', said by different speakers, of the same object, at the same time. They could very well both be true. Stevenson's concept of DISAGREEMENT IN ATTITUDE as distinct from DISAGREEMENT IN BELIEF enables one to explain the indubitable *opposition* between 'X is good' and 'X is not good' without regarding it as a case of logical contradiction. Attitudes may be opposed in the sense that those who have them may be led to adopt different courses of action with respect to something, one may seek to implement a policy another to oppose it. They do not contradict one another, but they may well be in conflict. From this point of view, what the subjectivist analysis of 'X is good' as 'I approve of X' fails to bring out is, not that 'X is good' is really a statement about X, but the way in which attitudes of approval may conflict with attitudes of non-approval.

Another matter into which emotivism offered new insight was the remarkable persistence of disputes about the definition of morally important terms like 'justice', 'courage', 'goodness', 'freedom', etc. On the face of it, questions about definitions ought not be hard to answer. There might be disagreements about how best to formulate a brief statement of a word's meaning, but we can surely not be ignorant of the meanings of words that are constantly on our lips. But, where words have both descriptive and emotive meaning, definition is bound to become a controversial matter. To be just, for instance, in the ordinary sense of the word, involves accepting as applying to oneself the rules or laws one would like applied to others, and, since the disposition to do this is admired, 'just' has a favourable emotive meaning and 'unjust' an unfavourable one. A person who does not admire what is ordinarily called just is, consequently, in a difficulty – to say that he is *against* justice, or *for* injustice, is to express both a favourable and an unfavourable attitude to the same thing. The least misleading thing to say in these circumstances is that one is against, not justice, but 'justice' (what is *called* justice), that is, in stating one's view, to try to dissociate the descriptive meaning of 'justice' from the emotive. Another manoeuvre is to say that the usual application of the term is mistaken, that 'justice' does not mean accepting as applying to oneself the rules that are applied to others, but rather, say, pursuing one's own interests to the limit of one's capacity. (Compare Thrasymachus' definition in Plato's *Republic* of 'justice' as the interest of the stronger party.) What has happened here is that an attempt has been made (whether consciously or not) to change the descriptive meaning of 'justice' while retaining its favourable emotive meaning. The effect of doing this may be to transfer the favourable attitudes expressed by the word from the sort of

F

conduct it originally described to the very different sort of conduct it describes when redefined. Definitions of this sort do not so much give the meanings of words as redirect attitudes. Hence, in Stevenson's phrase, they may be called 'PERSUASIVE DEFINITIONS'.

Examples of persuasive definitions include: Rousseau's claim that freedom is a matter, not of following appetites, but of obeying the laws laid down by society (people who favour subjection nearly always call it freedom); the application of the unfavourably emotive term 'waste' to any expenditure the author disapproves of in Veblen's *Theory of the Leisure Class*; the wide Marxist use of 'exploitation', according to which it can be said that workers in a capitalist economy are always exploited, regardless of the ways in which their incomes and conditions of life compare with those of other groups in their society.

It is arguable that the emotive theory was less valuable as a contribution to ethics than as an indication that a proper interest was being taken in non-cognitive (non-statement making) uses of language. In ethics the emotivists drew attention to a neglected function of moral judgements, their expressing and influencing of attitudes. Moral judgements were thought of as affecting attitudes causally, as means of operating upon or influencing attitudes. But it may seem that emotivists concentrated on some of the things moral judgements indisputably sometimes do to the neglect of what they are; that they took too little account of the possibility of moral judgements *telling* us something as distinct from merely *getting* us to do or feel something. The prescriptivists, whom we shall next consider, thought they could improve on emotivism in this respect, and also give an account of moral reasoning, which emotivism scarcely can.

PRESCRIPTIVISM

For the prescriptivist the model for moral judgements is, not the exclamation or interjection expressive of emotion or attitude, but the imperative; the imperative understood widely enough to cover, in addition to second person commands, resolves (statements of intention), and general commands or rules. There is a very wide range of locutions here brought together, and there are manifestly very many differences among them, but for prescriptivists they have significant features in common. They all relate to conduct in the sense that it can conform or fail to conform to them, and they are not primarily or necessarily vehicles for the expression of, or devices for influencing, emotion or attitude. Even the familiar second person command (the command proper), e.g. 'Start every question on a fresh sheet of paper', simply *tells* certain people to do a certain thing. It does not necessarily express a pro-attitude of the speaker towards the conduct prescribed – it is possible, though perhaps rare, for a speaker to want his command to be disobeyed, and if there is any impropriety in this it is still different from that involved in saying 'Ouch' when one is not hurt. And again, it is not part of the essence of a command that it should be causally effective or intended causally to bring about the action it prescribes. Commanding is not inciting. I may, knowing you to be counter-suggestible, say 'Do so and so' with the object of getting you to do the opposite. But I am still commanding or telling you to do it, though inciting you not to.

There is some possibility of giving an account of moral reasoning on prescriptivist lines, for imperatives, unlike interjections and exclamations, can figure in arguments much as statements can. From rules, such as 'There is to be no smoking in non-smoking compartments', together with particular premises, 'This is a non-smoking compartment', it certainly seems to follow that there is to be no smoking here. There may, as Aristotle pointed out, be practical as well as theoretical syllogisms, in which major premise and conclusion are imperatives (in a wide sense) not statements. There is at the present time acute controversy about the precise logical character of arguments involving imperatives, but of their possibility in some sense there is scarcely room for doubt.

The prescriptivist view is not that moral judgements *are* imperatives, but that they, in common with other value judgements, are in an important respect like them, and consequently that the study of imperatives is a useful starting point for moral philosophy.

Consider, first, the form of moral judgement that most resembles an imperative: 'You ought to do so and so'. It prescribes an action in much the same way as does the command 'Do so and so'. If so and so is not done, it seems natural to say of either locution that it has been disobeyed, but – significantly – it would be equally natural in the command case to say that the *speaker* has been disobeyed too, but not in the case of the moral judgement. The affinity between the moral judgement and command can be further brought out by reflecting that there is at least the appearance of contradiction in such remarks as 'You ought to do so and so, but do not' and 'I ought to do so and so, but I intend not to'. The thought here is that what contradicts a command must itself be akin to one. Of course, it is possible to think of more or less sensible interpretations of the apparently contradictory remarks, but it is also possible to do the same for such contradictory statements as 'It is raining and it is not raining'. It is common rhetorical device to secure emphasis by apparent self-contradiction. Let it be said, then, that the moral judgement 'You ought . . .' and the command 'Do . . .' have in common their prescriptive force, they both tell someone to do something. (I do not claim to have *shown* this; the present aim is to describe and illustrate views, not to justify any one of them.) What then is the difference between them? The prescriptivist suggestion is that it lies in the fact that 'You ought' is in a certain sense universal. Behind every grammatically singular 'You ought', there is a logically universal 'One ought'. If you ought to do so and so, then anybody whose situation is the same as yours ought to do the same sort of action. This is why 'You ought to fill in your income-tax return correctly, but I do not have to' is, not so much morally deplorable, as logically queer. Because of the implicit universality of locutions involving 'ought', 'You ought to . . . but I do not have to' is acceptable only if some relevant difference can be shown to exist between your situation and mine. In the income-tax case it is hard to see what relevant difference there could be, but in others it is easy enough. You (being rich) ought to contribute £50 to Oxfam, I (being poor) need not. I (having a child taking the examination) ought not to take part in marking the paper, you (having no personal interest in any candidate) may do so. You (as a Jew) may make anti-Semitic jokes, I (as a Gentile) ought not to.

Because of this universality, the 'ought' in 'You ought' does not relate solely to an individual act in a unique situation, but to acts of a certain type in situations of a certain type. For the same reason, ought-sentences in persons and tenses other than the second and present (or future) can have prescriptive force. 'He ought not to have done it' manifestly cannot be interpreted as commanding him not to have done so, but the universal rule behind it, that certain sorts of act in certain sorts of situation ought not to be done, refers to future acts as well as past ones. There is still, in this indirect way, the possibility of disobeying 'He ought not to have done it', despite its primarily referring to a past act.

Judgements involving 'good' have a feature which is analogous to the universality of 'ought'. If an object is deemed good then it follows that any relevantly similar object, and still more any qualitatively identical one, must be judged good too. It is incomprehensible that, for instance, a car should be good and an identical one not good. Of course, one Ford Cortina may be good while another is not, but then there will be some difference between them – one will have a defective casting, or will have been misassembled in some way. Hare, the most prominent prescriptivist, gives broadly similar accounts of both 'ought'-judgements and 'good'-judgements. *All* value judgements have in common prescriptivity and universalisability. More doubt has been expressed by critics about the prescriptivity than about the universalisability of 'good'. It is, perhaps, fair to say that prescriptivism is more plausible in relation to 'ought', cognitivism and more particularly naturalism in relation to 'good'. There are certainly very many differences among moral (and value) judgements, as well as between them and factual statements. Some disagreements in ethics derive from differences of emphasis or starting point.

I shall continue to concentrate on 'ought', but it must not be assumed that everything that applies to it can be uncontroversially transferred to 'good'.

The universality of 'ought' may be explained as deriving from the dependence of 'ought'-judgements upon reasons. We say you ought to do so and so *because*, for instance, you promised to do so, and the 'because' commits us to holding that in every other case in which a promise has been given (provided that there is no countervailing consideration) it ought to be carried out. The difference in point of universality between 'ought'-judgements and commands proper reflects the fact that reasons need to be given for the former in a way that they do not for the latter. The man who says 'Do this', and cannot or will not give a reason, possibly shows himself to be unreasonable, but he does not misuse the imperative verb form. The man who cannot or will not give a reason for 'You ought' – or at any rate, in order to allow for difficulties of formulating the reason, regards the request for reasons as irrelevant – arguably is misusing 'ought'. 'Ought'-judgements are passed in the light of standards. That is why, in complying with or flouting such judgements, we are not simply obeying or disobeying the speaker.

If, when we hear, 'You ought to do so and so', we know the standards that are being employed, it will be possible to work out something about the agent, his act and situation. This is true of every context, moral and non-moral, in which there are accepted standards. So, when the candidate is told that he ought to conclude his answers with a summary of the points made, we can infer that the practice is pleasing to examiners; when someone is told that he ought to pay back the money, we may infer that he has borrowed it with a promise of repayment. The extent and completeness of the information we thus obtain or can work out varies from context to context; it is sometimes considerable, sometimes minimal. Such information is often called the *descriptive meaning* of the 'ought'-judgement. (The same applies to judgements involving 'good'.)

'Descriptive meaning' is not a wholly satisfactory expression, since much of the information we may be able to collect when an 'ought'-judgement is made seems to be conveyed, not by the judgement itself, but by other features of the situation that we happen to notice. 'You ought to give the book to him' is a perfectly well-formed 'ought'-judgement that conveys very little information indeed. Nevertheless, misleading implications of the phrase 'descriptive *meaning*' are to a great extent counter-balanced when it is contrasted with 'PRESCRIPTIVE MEANING', and the latter held to be primary in the case of the words 'ought', 'right' and 'good'. 'Ought', in all its central uses, prescribes (perhaps indirectly via its universality) that something be done: its descriptive meaning, however, varies from context to context. Provided we grasp that so and so is being prescribed, we understand 'You ought to do so and so' even though we do not know its descriptive meaning. To know only the descriptive meaning in some context – that, for instance, so and so is something the law or the Church would have you do – is not understand the judgement. So with 'right' and 'ought', but not with, for instance, 'courage' or 'generosity'. In these cases it is the descriptive meaning that is primary. Calling an act courageous arguably does involve prescribing acts of that kind, but more importantly it is to state that it is of the kind. It is little, if at all, strange to say that an act, though courageous, should not have been performed. It is, in default of special explanations, contradictory to say a person should not do what he ought.

It will have been noticed that the prescriptive/descriptive meaning distinction resembles that between emotive and descriptive meaning. Prescriptivists are the heirs of the emotivists.

For prescriptivists, a moral judgement is – schematically – established by being brought under a standard (evaluative major premise) by means of a factual minor premise. Thus 'You ought to do so and so' would be justified by employing the factual minor 'You promised to do so and so' in order to bring it under the standard 'Promises ought to be kept'. (It is no part of the view that standards of moral value should be as simple and rigid as this: the maxims of the copy book or catechism, the ten commandments, the examples of the moral philosopher, are very imperfect indications of the complex and subtle standards that mature moralists actually employ.) Is prescriptivism, in the light of this account of justifying a moral judgement, objectivist or subjectivist? In so far as a factual minor premise is required, it may be claimed to be objectivist – what ought to be done depends on the ('objective') nature of the situation. Similarly, whether or not a thing is good will depend on whether it really does have the features which, in the light of the relevant standard, entitle us to judge it good. But what of the essential evaluative standards themselves? These, except possibly and partially in the case of the functional evaluations discussed at the end of chapter 5 (pages 70–1), are not dictated by the nature of the actions and things evaluated. They are rather, when ultimate, standards we choose to adopt. A subordinate standard may be justified by appeal to a superior standard that we accept, but there must clearly be a court of final appeal, a point at which we 'just' decide. Here the view parts company with objectivism, and fails to satisfy the widespread, but by no means certainly coherent, demand that morality should be, not a matter of human choice, but somehow founded in the nature of things.

There is scope for some conciliation here. Hare, who holds that choices of ultimate moral standards are logically open, has contended that these standards should be considered along with all the subordinate standards that fall under them, and indeed in the context of the whole ways of life to which they belong. Choice of moral standards there must be, he holds, but choices made with full knowledge of what one is choosing between cannot fairly be called arbitrary or non-rational. When everything, that conceivably could be, has been taken into account, it is preposterous to say that one who chooses does so for no reason at all. There will, I am sure, always be objectivists in ethics whom this will not satisfy: but I am almost equally sure that they are crying for the moon.

The prescriptivist can of course allow that there can be psychological and sociological explanations why people and cultures have the standards they do. There will be psychological and social limits within which our (logically) unlimited freedom of moral choice is (de facto) confined. Some naturalists in ethics think that moral standards can be deduced from psychological and sociological facts. The prescriptivist denies this, but does not also deny that these facts are in all respects irrelevant to morality. He holds that they come in by way of explanation rather than justification. If it is of the essence of naturalism to be this wordly (reject 'occult' properties) and to attach importance to the findings of the natural and social sciences, then the prescriptivist can join forces. It is only on the narrow question concerning the logical status of moral judgements that he parts company with the naturalist.

MORAL REASONING – UNIVERSALISABILITY

It is not easy, as we have already partly seen, for any view which stresses the uniqueness of moral (or value) judgements and their distinctness from factual statements, to account for more than the simplest sort of moral reasoning – the practical syllogism. What counts as a moral reason depends on the *content* of the moral standards we accept and that, within certain *de facto* limitations, depends on our choice. It might seem that we could support any moral conclusion we liked by simply adopting a suitable standard, that there is no logical limit to the standards we may choose to accept.

All this is true enough, but its impact can be somewhat reduced by emphasising the universal *form* (as opposed to the content) of moral standards, and the universality that this confers upon the moral judgements based upon them. Behind every 'You ought' or 'I ought' there is, as was pointed out above, a 'One ought' or an 'It ought to be'. And while there is virtually no limit, logical or factual, to what I may prescribe on a particular occasion, there is likely to be a limit to what I am prepared to prescribe universally. I am no doubt quite prepared to repudiate my debt to you, but if I am sensible, I will not want to prescribe debt repudiation universally, because that would be to prescribe that people should repudiate their debts to me. To use Kantian language, the moral test is never whether a proposed action is in my or anybody else's interest, but whether the maxim of the action (an action of that type) can be willed as a universal law.

There is, I think, little doubt that a good deal of moral argument depends on the universalisability of moral judgements. People who propose some course of conduct are told to reflect whether they would like it if others, or everybody, behaved in that way. And it is probable that such arguments are available in many cases in which we want the sympathetic imagination, or perhaps logical acumen and sheer information, to see that they are. The professional man who breaks two or three appointments in order to have an afternoon off may fail to see any resemblance between his conduct and what he condemns in the miner who misses a shift. Most of us who postpone paying bills when short of cash, feel righteously indignant when others fail to pay us on time. It is impossible to know how much moral agreement could be obtained if universalisation arguments were pushed to their limits, but their scope is obviously considerable, and, since universality is a fairly conspicuous and hopefully uncontroversial feature of moral judgements, it is tempting to place a good deal of weight in them in a morally divided society. There are many particular moral matters upon which we do not at the moment agree, but with universalisability we seem to have the possibility of agreeing on a method by which moral agreement might ultimately be reached.

It is no doubt significant that Hare, who has put great emphasis on the prescriptivity of moral judgements, and in consequence upon the element of logically open choice in morality, has also given almost equal weight to the universalisability of moral judgements.

How far will universalisability arguments take us in the direction of moral agreement? A doubt whether they can be effective by themselves arises from the fact that it seems to be possible always to satisfy the universality requirement in a merely formal sense. I claim the right to take a day off in order to play golf, but refuse to give you a day off for that purpose. You therefore complain that I am inconsistent (violate the universalisability requirement). To which I reply that our cases are different – and this is certainly a *relevant* rejoinder: universalisability requires only that people who are similarly situated have the same rights, not that everybody has, which would be absurd. But there will always be some difference between my situation and yours. It will always be possible to find some general description (perhaps beginning 'Man born on February 8th, 1928; 5 feet $10\frac{1}{2}$ inches tall; brown hair', etc.), which fits my case and not yours, and which therefore makes it possible for me to claim for all people covered by the description that they have a certain right without there being any danger of my allowing the right to you.

It is plain enough that not all differences between people's situations are held to be relevant from the moral point of view. The mere fact of having been born on different days is unlikely to be morally relevant in itself, nor is having different coloured hair. Differences of age, sex, status, however, frequently are held to be relevant, and the relevance of skin colour and racial type is, of course, controversial. I do not myself altogether despair of the possibility of giving some general account of the differences between people that are relevant from the moral point of view, though there are obvious difficulties of formulation and bound to be many points of dispute. The present contention is only that views about moral relevance are themselves moral views. If such views are needed before universalisability arguments can be made to work, then the relatively uncontroversial universalisability argument is of limited usefulness *by itself*. No doubt it is uncontroversial *because of* its limitations.

Universalisability considerations are frequently taken to point towards a rather down to earth social morality, which commits us to respecting the interests of others because we want them to respect ours. Possibly we should all like to promote our own interests at the expense of others, but that way chaos and conflict lie, so it pays us each to respect others' interests on the understanding that they will respect ours. The potential anti-Semite or racialist reflects that he would not like to be discriminated against and consequently recognises an obligation not to discriminate. But is it not both logically and in fact possible that someone might attach such importance to an ideal, or hate something so much, that he is prepared to have it promoted or attacked in opposition to his interests, even at the expense of his life? A dedicated communist caught out by a change in the party line might accept his punishment as just, much as a pious heretic in the ages of faith might have gone without resentment to the stake. The unfavourable word for such scorn of personal interest is 'fanaticism', and the complaint against the fanatic is, I suppose, that, while respecting the *form* of morality (universalisability), he neglects its substance (concern for human interests). I do not, myself enjoy so clear and distinct a notion of morality as to be able to say with confidence that the fanatic falls definitely outside its scope. Concern for human interests certainly is involved, but so frequently is scorn of them for the sake of principles. The idea of morality is complex and many sided, the emphasis may go here or there, and there are a variety of very different attitudes that have claims to be accounted moral.

THE MEANING OF 'MORAL'

We have been thinking of moral judgements as universal prescriptions expressed in sentences involving such words as 'good',
'right' and 'ought'. Various considerations, e.g. 'It will do harm',
'You promised' etc., are adduced in support of moral judgements,
and moral standards may be taken as indicating which considerations support what judgements. It is, however, clear that this
scheme of things – judgements, considerations, standards – fits a
much wider range of cases than would ordinarily be called moral.
It covers evaluation and appraisal generally, rather than moral
judgements in particular. It is needful, therefore, to ask what it is
about some judgements, considerations, standards that marks
them out as specifically moral.

Among the many suggestions that can be collected from ethical
literature, three at least stand out. To be moral, standards must
be in some way strictly universal, not subject to arbitrary exceptions or limitations of scope; moral standards must be conceived
as being of overriding importance, where they conflict with those
of other fields it is the moral that must prevail, morality may or
may not be good policy (expedient) but it is necessarily better
than any policy; moral standards have to do with the furtherance
of what are conceived to be human interests – the content of the
standards accepted as moral is generally explicable on this basis.
These three elements in the idea of morality fit well together. It
is because moral standards relate to abiding human interests that
they are conceived as universal and of paramount importance.
But the elements are nevertheless separable in principle and sometimes separated in fact. A fanatic may attach supreme importance
to something other than human interests. It is not quite clear
whether we should say that he repudiates morality altogether, or
merely that he embraces a one-sided or distorted version of it.
The same problem is presented by aesthetes. Do we say they
subordinate morality to aesthetics (goodness to beauty), or maybe
even abandon morality for the sake of aesthetics, or should we
rather say that the content of their morality is different from the
usual, that they make a sort of morality out of aesthetics (judge
things good because they are beautiful)? The judgements com-

monly passed on people's characters, as distinct from their actions, frequently have an aesthetic flavour. We tend to admire dedication, singleness of mind, courage, largely out of relation to the human good or ill produced by the bearers of such qualities. We have notions of nobility, greatness, honour, which are partly akin to, partly distinct from and potentially in conflict with, our moral ideals.

Different writers and schools in the history of ethics have stressed different aspects of morality. Utilitarians have been conspicuous in emphasising concern for human interests, the achieving of good results, sometimes with such disregard for universality (i.e. principle) as to invite charges of immorality. They have occasionally condoned secret violations by individuals of generally obligatory social rules, or even suggested that it is acceptable that the innocent be punished so long as it is generally believed that they are guilty − the deterrent effects of punishment depend, of course, on the *belief* rather than the fact that it is the guilty who are punished. Kant, at the other extreme (at least in his more theoretical moral writings), puts all the emphasis elsewhere, apparently advocating a scorn of humanly important consequence that is at once sublime and ridiculous, admirable and exasperating. It is tempting in face of such extremisms, to suppose that some middle way must be right, but this leaves out of account the elements of indeterminacy and tension in our idea of morality. There are a variety of points of view all with a claim to be called moral. There must be much that is common to them all, but the differences may be practically very important. The idea of morality, moreover, has a history and, no doubt, an as yet unspecifiable future. Present ideas develop from but are not identical with those of the past, future ideas will be different again.

It was noted previously in this chapter (pages 87–8) that, although the prescriptivist can give sense to the idea of giving reasons for moral judgements, he cannot fully satisfy the demand for objectivity in that he has to hold that ultimate standards of evaluation are not so much discovered as *chosen*. Though there may be a certain *de facto* consensus, which is doubtless explicable in psychological and sociological terms, there is no *logical* limit to the standards of value we may choose to adopt. But surely, it might be objected, there must be some limit to the standards which can be adopted as *moral*. The word 'moral' has some descriptive meaning which must preclude certain standards being counted as moral. This is true enough, but one of the outcomes of the attempt to specify the descriptive meaning of the word made earlier in the present section was a recognition of its open texture and inner tensions. There is a considerable measure of logically open choice *within* the idea of morality.

Is it also a logically open question whether we adopt the idea of morality at all? It has very frequently been thought that 'Why be moral?' is a question that moral philosophy ought to be able to answer, and felt to be both puzzling and scandalous that it has failed to do so to the general satisfaction. Of course, the import of the question depends on what 'moral' is taken to mean. If the word is allowed a specific descriptive meaning, the question will be logically open in the sense that it will be conceivable that someone should refuse to be moral. Morality will be a matter of being guided by a definite set of standards, and it will be accordingly possible to envisage a person's not being prepared to be so guided. On the other hand, if the element stressed in the meaning of 'moral' is that of overridingness, the question 'Why by moral?' hardly arises. To ask it is to ask whether a person is to be guided by the standards to which he attaches overriding importance, that is by the standards by which he *is* guided. A question which admits only of a vacuously affirmative answer is hardly a question at all.

Much of the difficulty that has been experienced in answering such questions as 'Why be moral?' thus derives from failure to decide exactly what 'moral' is to mean in the formulation of them. Answers which might be acceptable if the word is taken in one sense are clearly unacceptable if it is taken in another and, if it is not recognised that there are different senses involved, it will come to seem that no answer is possible at all.

A further, and fundamental, source of difficulty is that such questions may express demands for a species of *ultimate* justification that is necessarily unavailable in any field. The reasons for being moral must, it seems, be themselves either moral or not. If the former, then we have begged the question, which was why we should be guided by moral reasons at all: if the latter, then we have failed to answer it, for the question was quite precisely why we should be guided by moral as opposed to any other sort of reasons. (The situation is similar with regard to the justification of induction. 'Justifications' either themselves presuppose the soundness of inductive procedures or misrepresent induction as something else, e.g. a sort of deduction.) It is equally important to avoid both a moral scepticism founded on the recognition that that ultimate justifications are not to be had in morality *and*, on the other hand, moral credulity or complacency founded on the recognition that they are not to be had anywhere else either. There are limits to what can be accounted moral, but within these limits there is a range of logically open choice. This range can be reduced by making the descriptive meaning of 'moral' more determinate, but in proportion as this is done the scope for rejecting morality altogether is enlarged. There is a widespread demand for objectivity in morality which prescriptivism and non-cognitivism generally can conciliate but never finally satisfy. This is not necessarily a point against non-cognitivism. If one thinks, as I on the whole do, that the demand itself is unreasonable, it is a point in its favour.

THE FUTURE OF NON-COGNITIVISM

Until the present century cognitivism was in effect taken for granted. It was assumed that moral judgements had to be some sort of statement, and hence capable of truth and falsity, even by writers who emphasised features of moral judgements which would have been more readily intelligible on the basis that they were not statements at all. Cognitivism, however, as we have seen, faces great difficulties, and there is a feeling of liberation once the assumption that moral judgements must be statements is given up. There seems to be hope of avoiding the dilemmas of cognitivism by focusing on what moral judgements do – on their role in discourse. This the emotivists saw as a matter of their serving to express feelings or attitudes and causally to evoke them in others. But emotivism turns out to have very serious difficulties of its own and can be not unreasonably accused of neglecting what moral judgements *are* for the sake of what they can be used

for, or the result they may bring about. It cannot be of the essence
of moral judgements that they express emotions or attitudes.
though it is no doubt because they are what they are that they
tend to do these things. What they are, it is next suggested, are
prescriptions: either ways of telling, as opposed to getting, people
to choose or act, or at least logically relatable to rules, injunctions
and prohibitions. Prescriptivism is frequently misunderstood as
asserting that moral judgements are much more akin to second-
person commands than its proponents intend to assert, and much
of the criticism it has attracted is founded on misunderstanding.
It is no part of the view that all moral judgements perform the
same speech act, that they prescribe in a sense opposed to advise,
counsel, commend, etc. 'Prescribe' is used, perhaps contrary to
usage, as a general term for a great variety of speech acts, which
have many differences among them as well as one thing (guiding
action) in common. There is no reason in principle why prescriptivists should not emphasise the differences, and some have.
It is not by any means certain that prescriptivism has received the
full development it is capable of, but there are already some signs
of a cognitivist counter revolution. Progress in philosophy is not
a matter of one sort of view permanently overcoming all rivals.
Discredited types of view simply go underground for a period
and then re-emerge on a new level of sophistication. The new
cognitivism, if that indeed is what is coming, will be free of some
of the defects of earlier varieties, but even so is unlikely to prove
permanently satisfactory. No branch of moral philosophy will
ever be complete.

SUMMARY

Ethical rationalism and naturalism both assume that moral judgements
are statements. Non-cognitivist views deny this, and consequently
maintain the 'autonomy of ethics', the gulf between (moral) value and
fact.

The emotive theory of ethics is the view that moral judgements are
primarily expressions of feeling or attitude. The importance, and
difficulty, of drawing a firm distinction between expressing feelings and
saying that one has them. Disagreement in attitude and disagreement
in belief. Persuasive definition.

Prescriptivism selects the imperative rather than the interjection as as a reference point for the study of moral judgements. Moral judgements as not singular but universal prescriptions. Prescriptive and descriptive meaning of moral terms and judgements. Prescriptive meaning of 'ought', 'right' and 'good' is primary. The extent to which prescriptivism allows for the objectivity of moral judgements. Ultimate standards of evaluation chosen but, arguably, not arbitrarily or non-rationally. Moral standards are not derivable from the findings of psychology and sociology, but psychological and sociological explanations can be given why we choose the standards we do.

Universalisability as the basis of moral reasoning. No one is morally at liberty to do anything he is not prepared to have anybody else do whose situation is relevantly similar. Views about what is relevantly similar, are, however, moral views. The social morality of respecting one another's interests. Morality presumptively, but not necessarily exclusively, social.

What is the difference between moral and other sorts of standards of evaluation? Universality, overriding importance, reference to human interests. These three are naturally associated, but separable in principle and sometimes in fact. Fanatics and aesthetes. The idea of morality is complex and there are tensions within it, hence the difficulty of the question 'Why be moral?'.

Non-cognitivism has been dominant for a time, but there are signs that a cognitivist revival is about due.

FURTHER READING

For a classical, if polemical and over-brief, exposition of the emotive theory, see Ayer (2, chapter 6). Also Stevenson (65, 66). Criticisms of the theory are to be found in most general works on ethics. See also Stroll (67) and, for an early version of the theory, Ogden and Richards (45).

For persuasive definition, see Stevenson (65, 66). For prescriptivism, the best source is Hare (18, 19). Some criticisms are very clearly expressed in Warnock (69).

On the meaning of 'moral', apart from Hare and Warnock, see Wilson (72, part 1) and Hart (20, chapter 8).

On the question 'Why be moral?', see Bradley (5, chapter 2) and Baier (4, chapter 12). Prichard's discussion in (53, chapter 1) is also relevant.

7 Morality, Science and Religion

This book began with the discussion of certain problems that were internal to morality and then moved on to consider very general philosophical or logical questions about the status of moral judgements. It is time now to give attention to the frontiers of morality, to its relation to other fields of thought and concern, in particular science and religion. There are still a great many, and have been more, who think that morality hardly makes sense outside a religious framework, and there are a growing number who think that science should supersede religion in this regard.

First, then, what scope is there for a scientific morality?

On some naturalistic views of moral judgements there could be a scientific morality in the strong sense that moral judgements would actually be part of science. They could, as statements of fact (empirical statements), appear as the conclusions of scientific arguments. On prescriptivist and, indeed, non-cognitivist views generally, however, moral judgements will be radically different from any sort of scientific statement. But, very different in principle though the relations between morality and science must be on these two sorts of view, there are nevertheless some similarities in practice. Even though for prescriptivists there cannot properly speaking be a scientific morality, there are still, as will appear below, a variety of ways in which the findings of science are relevant to morality. And for many views which are in form naturalistic the element of indeterminacy is so great as, in effect, to leave scope for something approaching autonomous moral judgement. To a prescriptivist it is *logically* open what ultimate moral principles we adopt although, people being what they are, the commoner choices will fall within a fairly narrow range. But for a naturalist, who holds that to say that a practice is morally commendable is equivalent to saying, for example, that it makes for human happiness or promotes human interests, the non-scientific questions what to count as happiness or interests loom as large as the scientific questions how to obtain or promote whatever we take them to be.

There is a temptation, whatever opinion be held about the status of moral judgements, to take a simple, means/end view of the relations between science and morality. It is true that we often do think in means/end terms about moral matters, for example, about sexual conduct. We set up a notion of what is valuable in human relations and applaud or condemn modes of behaviour according as they do or do not tend to bring about the end. In setting before ourselves ends, we are making moral or other sorts of value judgements, but questions about means (how to obtain the ends) are matter of fact and, in principle, scientific. Though ultimate values will be extra-scientific, the backing for subordinate or derived moral judgements will be scientific, and moral opinions can be held to improve in rationality as common-sense beliefs, or superstitions, about what leads to what are replaced by properly scientific ones. Problems of morality, education, politics seem thus capable of becoming, like those of medicine, matters of applied science. In Mill's words, 'The reasons of a maxim of policy, or of any other rule of art, can be nothing but the theorems of the corresponding science'.

There are, however, at least two reasons for holding this attractively clear view to be over-simple. The first is that it is exceptional for ends to be highly determinate and valued by practically everyone, and to take it to be the norm is consequently misleading. In such cases there really is nothing more than a question in appplied science, what has to be done to get what, a technical question. But morality (and for that matter even economics) requires the adoption of a wider point of view. Since what needs to be done in order to achieve one end may frustrate the achievement of other more important ones, means have to be evaluated as well as ends. Technical questions are relatively easy because we make them so by ignoring all sorts of considerations and complications that are practically important. Economic questions are somewhat harder because a wider, though still limited, range of considerations is taken into account. Moral questions are in this way hardest of all, for nothing that bears upon human interests can be ignored.

It should be a platitude or truism that the end justifies the means for, obviously, nothing could be valuable as a means unless something were valued as an end. But in fact the dictum is often condemned as Machiavellian, Jesuitical or otherwise immoral. This is because it is interpreted as licensing any sort of behaviour whatever provided only that it is a means to something we happen to want; as, that is to say, reducing every practical question to a merely technical one.

The second reason for doubting the adequacy of a simple means/end picture of evaluation is closely akin to the first. The picture fits the specialised arts fairly well. The rules of good driving, even perhaps those of medicine, are justifiable as tending to promote fairly determinate ends. It is not, of course, very easy to say positively what health is, but there are a great many conditions that are uncontroversially incompatible with it, and to a great extent medicine consists in trying to prevent such conditions coming about or to eliminate them if they have done so. But the ends of such 'higher' arts (if that is the word) as 'education', 'politics', 'morality', are so indeterminate that their rules or maxims are perhaps better regarded as constituting or defining them than as pointing the way to ends that can be independently conceived. In these areas we are likely to be more confident about procedures than aims or goals. From this point of view utilitarianism, for instance, which sets up the greatest happiness of the greatest number as the end of morality, is empty and unenlightening rather than mistaken. It is not that it clearly specifies something that is not the end of morality, but rather that it fails to specify any definite end at all. It is almost as enlightening to say that the general happiness is whatever is produced by morally commendable courses of conduct, as that those courses of conduct which produce general happiness are morally commendable. Kant, with his insistence that the imperatives of morality are categorical not hypothetical, can be read as making this type of protest against utilitarian, means/end conceptions of morality. And, much more recently and in a different field, the same sort of point lies behind Peters' claim that educational values are not so much goals to be aimed at as rules of procedure.

Whatever view we take of the scope of means/end conceptions of practical thinking, there are other ways that science is relevant that we must recognise. If morality relates primarily to conduct, scientific studies of the world in which we have to act can hardly be ignored. They offer us, for instance, potentially exact knowledge of what is and is not on in the way of behaviour. ('Ought' implies 'can'.) There is no point in enjoining people to do what they cannot, or prohibiting what they cannot help. Naïve, pre-scientific moralists are notoriously prone to see people as predominantly wicked, as failing to do what is right and persisting in what is wrong. But the trouble could well be that the moralist's expectations are unrealistic. This seems to me the main moral relevance of such studies of actual conduct as the Kinsey reports on sexual behaviour. It cannot be argued that something is right because everybody does it – morality is not custom – but it is obvious that widespread practices are unlikely to be given up easily or quickly, which does raise a doubt about the practical point of condemning them. The precepts of morality will not coincide with actual conduct. They could not function as guides to conduct if they did. But equally they can only guide conduct within the limits of the psychologically and sociologically possible, and need therefore to be framed in the light of what those limits are.

Another way in which social science might be relevant to morality (although this is still a matter of defining the limits within which we have to choose) is by clarifying the interrelationships between factors in society. Changes in one area may produce consequential changes in others. The economic emancipation of women and teenagers will have effects on marriage and patterns of family life. There may even be the inverse relationship between sexual expression and aggression implied in the agreeable injunction to make love not war. One should not exaggerate the extent of the knowledge we already possess. There are few well-established large-scale conclusions in social science, possibilities may be wishfully exploited, and since where human conduct is concerned thinking largely makes things so, ill-evidenced speculations may be self-verifying. All the same, when every doubt is given due weight, there is still ample need for moralists to pay attention to social science.

Science is not, of course, simply the study of the world in which we act. It, or its application, is also a great force for changing it. New developments and discoveries present new objects for moral appraisal. At the individual level are such things as contraception, artificial insemination, transplant surgery. On a larger scale, the dramatic reduction in the infant death rate and the remarkable progress made in 'death control' generally, raise doubts about the appropriateness of the long-established enthusiasm for pro-creation; developments in weapon technology raise doubts about traditional attitudes to warfare and national independence; developments in communications and opinion control raise doubts about political democracy.

Innovations such as these make it hard to see how morality can remain stable at the level of detailed precepts and present special difficulties for authoritarian conceptions of it. Courts of law, when they have to deal with issues unforeseen by legislators, tend to stretch the law, enlarge the old definitions, to cover the new cases. Rule-bound moralists sometimes proceed in the same way. They try to bring artificial insemination, for example, under the established ban on adultery, or consider abortion, and even some forms of contraception, as species of homicide. There are grave objections to this. It may very well mean that new issues are settled less happily than they might be if we took a long, cool look at them in the light of our own more general values. And, perhaps more importantly, it may bring it about that practices which have great importance in relation to those values escape moral assessment altogether, because they do not fall within the scope of received moral rules. It is very doubtful indeed whether very large families are any longer acceptable in an increasingly crowded and hungry world, but how many children to have still tends not to be thought of as a moral question at all.

It was argued in an earlier chapter that morality cannot be identified with any set of currently accepted rules (i.e. with positive morality). The present considerations support that argument. There is, moreover, a clear implication for moral education which, so far from being a matter of training people to conform to accepted rules, must seek to inculcate in them the capacity critically to assess accepted rules and current practices by reference to abiding general values.

FREEDOM AND DETERMINISM

There is a further way in which science might be thought to have a bearing on morality. It is very different from those considered in the previous section and, while it cannot be adequately treated in a short space, it can hardly be ignored altogether.

DETERMINISM, usually interpreted as the thesis that every event (including every human action) has a cause, or sometimes that every event is predictable in principle or scientifically explicable, is frequently thought *both* to be rendered more credible by the progress of science *and* to be incompatible with moral freedom and responsibility. To give a scientific explanation of an event seems to be a matter of showing, given certain facts and established laws, that it had to happen as it did. But morality, if its injunctions and assessments are to have any point, requires that there be alternative acts equally open to the agent, that sometimes at least he could act differently from the way he does. It is clear that at present we do not know the causes, or explanations, of very many types of event, but there seems to be no limit to the extent to which they may become known, and hence that, if determinism really is incompatible with freedom, the area in which there may be freedom diminishes as science develops.

Moral freedom was considered in chapter 4 above. There an attempt was made to present a notion of freedom and responsibility (the opposite of compulsion and ignorance) which would be compatible with any likely sort of determinism. I shall not try to add to that account of freedom here, only to suggest that determinism is both more mysterious and less certainly incompatible with freedom than its advocates suppose.

Any form of determinist thesis is, presumably, a synthetic universal proposition of unlimited scope. It is very difficult indeed to see how there ever could be adequate grounds for supposing such a proposition true. In believing it, as many of us are unquestionably inclined to do, we go way beyond any conceivable evidence. Nor is it certainly correct to hold that all science is deterministic in the sense of seeking, or at any rate *finding*, strictly universal laws. The general statements of social science are typically statistical, relating to the behaviour or characteristics of such-and-such a percentage or proportion of a group rather than to that of all the members of it. It is, however, sometimes hoped that behind such imperfect first approximations there are strictly universal laws waiting to be discovered. But is this reasonable? It appears that in sub-atomic physics the laws are *irreducibly* statistical, that uncertainty, indeterminism, is, so to say, present in the bedrock facts themselves. It is not surprising that moralists who are worried by determinism have found some solace here, though, in fact, the implications of physical indeterminism for the sort of determinism that presents a difficulty for moral freedom are very hard to assess. Indeterminism at the sub-atomic level is compatible with determinism at the level of large-scale phenomena to which explanations of human actions belong.

There are formidable speculative difficulties to be overcome before the rights and wrongs of determinism can be sorted out. It seems incredible that we should have to wait for their resolution before we are entitled to believe in so practical a matter as moral freedom. This seems to me to be an important point in favour of the workday notion of freedom and responsibility developed in chapter 4.

Moreover, it seems possible that some of the difficulties determinism is felt to present for moral freedom derive from misunderstandings of cause, (scientific) law, and kindred notions. Causes, however the term is formally defined, are thought of as compulsions, as making their effects happen. Scientific laws are thought of as coercive, somewhat as the laws of the land would be if the police were 100 per cent efficient. It is easy to see, when focusing directly on the issues, that these misunderstandings are absurd, but much harder to exclude them altogether from one's thinking. They are a formidable obstacle to allowing that freedom and responsibility may be compatible with causation, scientific explanation, determinism generally.

For my own part I am not yet persuaded that there is any reason for abandoning the view, deriving from Hobbes and Hume, that causation ('properly' understood, of course) is compatible with freedom (again 'properly' understood). Sometimes, it is true, the excessive claim has been made that 'free', when applied to an action, means 'caused by volition (or desire)', i.e. that, far from being incompatible with causation, freedom actually entails it. This view, after a long innings, has fairly recently come under suspicion. There are general reasons from the philosophy of mind, involving the relation between mind and body, for doubting whether volitions or desires could be causes of actions. And it has been questioned on logico-linguistic grounds whether the 'if' in 'He would have acted differently *if* he had chosen (wanted to)' – a phrase often offered as an analysis of 'He acted freely' – is correctly regarded as conditional or causal. But the moral I draw here is that one sort of compatibility view of freedom and determinism has been shown to be inadequate, not that any compatibility view has been excluded in principle.

The most promising approach seems to me to be to start from the idea that there are at least two different, but not necessarily incompatible or competitive, ways of explaining what people do. On the one hand, we may explain the *movements* they make (it is perhaps unnatural to speak of 'actions' here) by citing causes, maybe of a neurological or physiological character. On the other, we explain their *actions* by reference to the purposes they have and their beliefs about what has to be done in order to realise them. The distinction may be said to be between causal explanations of people's *reactions* (movements), and purposive explanations of their actions. Causal explanations tend to generate worries about freedom and responsibility. Purposive ones do not. Traditional compatibility views tend to over-assimilate purposive explanations to causal ones (e.g. by treating volitions or motives as causes), but such errors are no necessary part of the compatibility approach.

If the distinction between causal and purposive explanations is accepted, it will then come to seem possible that some of the social sciences offer purposive rather than causal explanations. In economics, the thought sometimes seems to be that people have certain purposes and that what they do is explicable as what they believe, or what a rational person would believe, needs to be done in order to achieve them. Psycho-analytical explanations too, it seems, may be of this kind, though there is the formidable complication that the purposes are held to be unconscious. And some sociological explanations may be of the same order. In so far as the social sciences offer explanations that approximate to the purposive rather than the causal model, their continued development should not provoke new worries about freedom and responsibility.

It is obviously impossible to throw much light on the vast complex of questions concerning freedom and determinism in the last chapter of a short introduction to moral philosophy. But not to have mentioned it at all would have left a misleadingly narrow impression of the theoretical scope of the subject. For some philosophers, Kant for instance, the major questions of moral philosophy are to be found here.

MORALITY AND RELIGION

This too is an enormous topic. I shall confine myself to saying something about the logical relations between science and religion, i.e. the question whether there can be a religious morality in a sense corresponding to that in which, for naturalists, there can be a scientific one. I shall ignore questions of free-will (though the idea of an omnipotent and omniscient God raises difficulties at least as profound as those raised by deterministic science) and the so-called problem of evil (i.e. the question whether the evil in the world can be reconciled with the existence of an all-powerful and benevolent God). I assume as obvious that the content of our current moral code has been greatly influenced by centuries of Christianity, and that a further decline in religious belief and practice (I make no predictions here) would be likely to lead to changes in content. It would also produce changes in attitude. For believers, morality has an extra-terrestrial dimension, its requirements have an ultimate importance that those of a mundane social morality inevitably lack. (Kant is the only, mainly secular, writer who does much to remedy this lack. Hence his considerable appeal to those whose moral teaching began in a religious context, i.e. nearly all of us, whatever our present religious belief.)

The main theoretical objection to a scientific morality, that moral judgements as values are not derivable from matters of fact, has also been employed against the idea of a religious morality. Religious belief, as traditionally conceived, includes assenting to certain propositions, about the existence and nature of God, His role as creator and sustainer of the universe, and so forth. These propositions purport to state facts, even if not empirical facts. If moral judgements, not being factual, cannot appear as the conclusions of scientific arguments, then, by the same token, they cannot appear as conclusions of religious arguments either. Morality, if autonomous, is equally distinct from and independent of science and religion – a position disappointing to those believers who want to subordinate morality to religion, to argue that it does not make sense to think of morality apart from religion, but encouraging to others who want rather to proceed to religion by way of morality. Certainly, if it is desired to argue from morality to religion, morality must be allowed to be capable of standing up by itself, otherwise there is no firm starting point.

There are great attractions in conceiving the relationship between religion and morality in fact/value terms on the analogy of that between science and morality. It opens up the possibility of communication and agreement between believers and unbelievers in moral matters. It allows believers to discuss practical moral issues without bringing in specifically religious considerations (e.g. references to scriptural teaching) which are inevitably divisive. And it permits the would-be secular moralist with no taste for religious controversy to dispute the logical relevance of religion without having to declare himself on the acceptability or otherwise of religious claims.

But, genuinely attractive though it is, it is to be feared that this account of the relationship between religion and morality is too simple.

In the first place, views about religion and morality cannot be developed in complete independence of each other. It had to be allowed in the course of the discussion of naturalism in chapter 5 (pages 70–1), that there would be more scope for a sort of functional naturalism if it could be maintained that people and their actions were intended to serve purposes not their own. A person unpersuaded by religious claims has good reason for rejecting that sort of naturalism, but he cannot without circularity at the same time make his rejection of it a reason for rejecting religious morality. It is hardly surprising that, if, as we have on the whole done, we consider morality out of all relation to religion, we shall come to think that religion is logically irrelevant to it. In moral philosophy, as in other branches of the subject, it is rare to find conclusive arguments for any position. Often what tips the balance is a very inconsiderable factor indeed, which could easily be transferred to the other scale by taking a wider point of view. We cannot – and this is the only point I want to emphasise here – settle the relationship between religion and morality by considering either in isolation from the other.

The second point is that it cannot be taken for granted that religious locutions are statements of fact. Traditionally it has certainly been so supposed, but the force of this is weakened by the fact that this has traditionally been supposed, if only by default of explicitly considering the issue, in virtually all fields. We saw above how, once attention was given to this question in relation to moral judgements, it proved possible to develop non-cognitivist analyses of them that were at least plausible. It is perhaps easier to make sense of morality on a non-cognitivist than on a cognitivist basis. But the difficulties of cognitivism in philosophy of religion are certainly no less than those of its counterpart in ethics. There is ample reason for developing non-cognitivist analyses of religious locutions, and certain writers (Braithwaite, Robinson) have attempted to do so. Acceptance of such a view would, as Braithwaite insists, have important implications for the relationship between religion and morality. A religious morality would be possible, not because moral judgements were held (as by naturalists) to be statements of fact, but for the opposite reason that religious locutions were held to be akin to value judgements.

CONCLUDING NOTE

I have deliberately chosen to end this chapter on a problematic note. Philosophy is never finished, no problem is finally solved, though there are solid gains to be obtained from surveying tracts of philosophical argumentation. It was in the belief that this is so that I began by trying to convey something of the range and content of moral philosophy. There is, perhaps, precious little established doctrine, but some acquaintance with its problems and distinctions is a means to clear thought about problems of conduct. There are two points that I have throughout sought to emphasise above all others – one about morality, the other about moral philosophy. The former is that moral thinking is continuous with rational thinking generally; the latter that moral philosophy is continuous with the rest of philosophy.

SUMMARY

On naturalistic views of moral judgements they could actually form part of science, on prescriptivist views they are autonomous. In practice, the contrast between different views of moral judgements in relation to the possibility of a scientific morality is not so great.

Means/end approaches to the relations between science and morality have limitations. From the moral point of view, means must be evaluated as well as ends. Moral rules define or constitute the end of morality, and do not simply point the way to it.

Science is relevant to morality in helping to define the limits within which we have to choose. Innovations of various sorts present new objects for moral assessment.

The development of science does not inevitably lend credence to determinism as a general thesis. Nor is determinism necessarily incompatible with moral freedom and responsibility. Causal and purposive explanations contrasted. Some social sciences seem to offer purposive explanations, and consequently do not raise worries about freedom.

If religious locutions are conceived as statements of fact, there are the same objections to religious as to scientific morality. It is not, however, certain that they should be so conceived. On non-cognitivist

H

accounts, religious locutions could be of the same logical status as moral judgements.

FURTHER READING

For the possibility of a scientific morality the literature cited in connection with chapter 5, especially pages 57–64, above is relevant. For means/end accounts of morality, see Hume (25) and Mill (39, Book VI, chapter 12). For criticisms of such accounts, see Kant (29) and Prichard (53, chapter 1). For criticisms of means/end approaches to education, see Peters (47).

On freedom and determinism, see Hume (24, section 8), Ayer (3, chapter 12), Cranston (11) and Hook (22). On purposive explanations, see Peters (46).

On religion and morality, Moore (43) is relevant. There is a useful discussion too in MacBeath (36). For non-cognitivist accounts of religious belief, see Braithwaite (6), Robinson (57) and Hare in Mitchell (41).

Bibliography

Note: There are no established doctrines in moral philosophy, nor indeed in any other branch of the subject. Moral philosophy cannot be defined by formulating a set of first principles, but only, if at all, by referring to a set of classic texts. The books marked with an asterisk in the list below have a special claim to be considered definitive of the subject, and are indispensable reading for the serious student.

Books

1. *Aristotle *Nichomachean Ethica* (many translations)
2. Ayer, A. J. *Language, Truth and Logic* (Gollancz. Second edition 1946)
3. Ayer, A. J. *Philosophical Essays* (Macmillan 1963)
4. Baier, K. *The Moral Point of View* (Cornell University Press (USA) 1958)
5. Bradley, F. H. *Ethical Studies* (Oxford University Press 1962. First Edition 1876)
6. Braithwaite, R. B. *An Empiricist's View of Religious Belief* (Cambridge University Press 1955)
7. Brandt, R. B. *Hopi Ethics* (University of Chicago Press 1954)
8. Brandt, R. B. *Ethical Theory* (Prentice-Hall 1959)
9. *Butler, J. *Fifteen Sermons* (Second edition with Preface 1729, most recent edition: Matthews, W.R. (Ed.) Bell 1949)
10. Carritt, E. F. *Ethical and Political Thinking* (Oxford University Press 1947)
11. Cranston, M. *Freedom: A New Analysis* (Longmans 1953)
12. D'Arcy, E. *Human Acts* (Oxford University Press 1963)
13. Ewing, A. C. *Second Thoughts in Moral Philosophy* (Routledge & Kegan Paul 1959)
14. Flew, A. G. N. *Evolutionary Ethics* (Macmillan 1967)
15. Flügel, J. C. *Man, Morals and Society* (Duckworth 1945)
16. Freud, S. *New Introductory Lecturers on Psychoanalysis* (Hogarth Press 1962)

17. Ginsberg, M. *Essays in Sociology and Social Philosophy* Vols I–III (Heinemann 1947–61)

18. Hare, R. M. *The Language of Morals* (Oxford University Press 1952)

19. Hare, R. M. *Freedom and Reason* (Oxford University Press 1963)

20. Hart, H. L. A. *The Concept of Law* (Oxford University Press 1961)

21. Hart, H. L. A. *Punishment and Responsibility* (Oxford University Press 1968)

22. Hook, S. (Ed.) *Determinism and Freedom* (Collier Books 1961)

23. Hospers, J. *Introduction to Philosophical Analysis* (Routledge & Kegan Paul. Second edition 1967)

24. Hume, D. *Enquiry concerning Human Understanding* (1748 many editions)

25. *Hume, D. *Enquiry concerning the Principles of Morals* (1751 many editions)

26. Hutcheson, F. see selection in Selby-Bigge (61).

27. Huxley, J. S. & Huxley, T. H. *Evolution and Ethics* (Pilot Press 1947)

28. Kant, I. *Critique of Pure Reason* (1781, translated Kemp Smith, Macmillan 1929)

29. *Kant, I. *Groundwork to the Metaphysic of Morals* (1785 many translations)

30. Kant, I. 'On the Supposed Right to Tell a Lie' (in *Kant's Theory of Ethics*, Abbott, Sixth edition 1909. Also contains translation of *Groundwork*).

31. Kaufmann, F. *Methodology of the Social Sciences* (Oxford University Press 1944)

32. Ladd, J. *The Structure of a Moral Code* (Harvard University Press 1957)

33. Lamont, W. D. *The Principles of Moral Judgment* (Oxford University Press 1946)

34. Lyons, D. *The Forms and Limits of Utilitarianism* (Oxford University Press 1965)

35. Mabbott, J. D. *Introduction to Ethics* (Hutchinson 1966)

36. MacBeath, A. *Experiments in Living* (Macmillan 1952)

37. MacIntyre, A. C. *A Short History of Ethics* (Collier-Macmillan 1966)

38. Mead, M. *Sex and Temperament in Three Primitive Societies* (William Morrow (USA) 1963. Routledge 1935)

39. Mill, J. S. *System of Logic* (Longmans. Eighth edition 1898, sixth impression 1956)

40. *Mill, J. S. *Utilitarianism* (1861) and Liberty (1859) (Dent 1962)

41. Mitchell, B. (Ed.) *Faith and Logic* (Allen & Unwin 1957)

42. Mitchell, B. *Law, Morality and Religion* (Oxford University Press 1967)

43. *Moore, G. E. *Principia Ethica* (Cambridge University Press 1959)

44. Nowell-Smith, P. H. *Ethics* (Penguin 1954)

45. Ogden, C. K. & Richards, I. A. *The Meaning of Meaning* (Kegan Paul 1923)

46. Peters. R. S. *The Concept of Motivation* (Routledge & Kegan Paul 1958)

47. Peters, R. S. *Authority, Responsibility and Education* (Allen & Unwin 1959)

48. Peters, R. S. *Ethics and Education* (Allen & Unwin 1966)

49. Piaget, J. *The Moral Judgment of the Child* (Routledge & Kegan Paul 1960)

50. *Plato *Meno* (many editions including Penguin)

51. *Plato *Republic* (many editions including Penguin)

52. Price, R. see selection in Selby-Bigge (61).

53. Prichard, H. *Moral Obligation* (Oxford University Press 1949)

54. Prior, A. N. *Logic and the Basis of Ethics* (Oxford University Press 1949)

55. Raphael, D. D. *The Moral Sense* (Oxford University Press 1947)

56. Raphael, D. D. *Moral Judgment* (University of London Press 1954)

57. Robinson, J. *Honest to God* (SCM Press 1963)

58. Ross, W. D. *The Right and the Good* (Oxford University Press 1930)

59. Ross, W. D. *The Foundations of Ethics* (Oxford University Press 1939)

60. Schilpp, P. A. (Ed.) *The Philosophy of G. E. Moore* (Evanston University Press (USA) 1942)

61. Selby-Bigge (Ed.) *British Moralists* (Dover paperback 1965)

62. Sidgwick, H. *The Methods of Ethics* (Macmillan 1963)

63. Sidgwick, H. *Outlines of the History of Ethics* (Macmillan. Sixth edition 1962)

64. Spencer, H. *The Principles of Ethics* (Williams & Norgate 1892–3)

65. Stevenson, C. L. *Ethics and Language* (Yale University Press (USA) 1944)

66. Stevenson, C. L. *Facts and Values* (Yale University Press (USA) 1963)

67. Stroll, A. *The Emotive Theory of Ethics* (California University Press 1954)

68. Toulmin, S. E. *The Place of Reason in Ethics* (Cambridge University Press 1950)

69. Warnock, G. J. *Contemporary Moral Philosophy* (Macmillan 1967)

70. Waddington, C. H. *The Ethical Animal* (Allen & Unwin 1960)

71. Whiteley, C. H. & Whiteley, W. M. *The Permissive Morality* (Methuen 1964)

72. Wilson, J., Williams, N. & Sugarman, B. *Introduction to Moral Education* (Penguin 1967)

73. Wootton, B. *Crime and the Criminal Law* (Stevens 1963)

There will in due course be a volume on most types of ethical theory in the Macmillan series, *New Studies in Ethics* edited by W. D. Hudson.

Articles

74. Atkinson, R. F. & Williams, B. 'Consistency in Ethics', *Aristotelean Society Supplementary Volume*, **39** (1965)

75. Gardiner, P. 'On Assenting to a Moral Principle', *Aristotelean Society Proceedings*, **55** (1954–5)

76. Mabbott, J. D. & Horsburgh, H. J. H. 'Prudence', *Aristotelean Society Supplementary Volume*, **36** (1962)

77. MacLagan, W. G. 'How Important is Moral Goodness?' *Mind*, **64** 254 (April 1955)

78. Strawson. P. F. 'Social Morality and Individual Ideal', *Philosophy*, **36** (January 1961)

79. Urmson, J. O. 'Saints and Heroes', *Essays in Moral Philosophy* Melden A. I. (Ed.) (Washington University Press 1958)

80. Whiteley, C. H. 'On Duties', *Aristotelean Society Proceedings*, **53** (1952–3)

Collections

Many useful articles and selections from older and more recent books are to be found in the following volumes.

81. Brandt, R. B. (Ed.) *Value and Obligation* (Harcourt, Brace & World 1961)

82. Foot, P. (Ed.) *Theories of Ethics* (Oxford University Press 1967)

83. Margolis, J. *Contemporary Ethical Theory* (Random House (USA) 1966)

84. Melden, A. I. *Ethical Theories* (Prentice Hall 1955)

85. Sellars, W. & Hospers, J. *Readings in Ethical Theory* (Appleton-Century-Crofts (USA) 1952)

Glossary

Note: Terms which are fully discussed in the text are not necessarily defined in the glossary.

ABSOLUTISM. The view that moral standards or principles are valid universally, that their content and authority does not vary according to the circumstances in which they apply, and that they admit of no exceptions. (Cf. relativism.)

ALTRUISM (ETHICAL). The view that morality requires one to give *greater* weight to other people's welfare than to one's own. (Cf. egoism, neutralism.)

ANALYTIC. A statement is said to be analytic if its negation is contradictory; e.g. the statement 'Triangles have three sides', is analytic because its negation, 'There is a triangle which has not got three sides', is contradictory. Analytic statements are necessary (necessarily true), true on logical (as opposed to factual or empirical) grounds, true *a priori*. Statements which are not analytic are synthetic (q.v.).

A POSTERIORI STATEMENT. A statement of which the truth or falsity can be ascertained only empirically (i.e. by observation or experiment). *A posteriori* statements are consequently synthetic and contingent (q.v.).

A PRIORI STATEMENT. A statement which is not *a posteriori* or empirical.

AUTONOMY OF ETHICS. In recent moral philosophy, the view: 1. that moral terms like 'good', 'right', 'ought', cannot be defined purely descriptively or factually; and 2. that moral judgements cannot be deduced from premises which do not include moral judgements. More generally upholders of the autonomy of ethics maintain that morality is a subject in its own right, not reducible to science, religion, custom, etc.; they are likely also to maintain that in moral action the will is free.

CATEGORICAL IMPERATIVE. Kant's principle that one ought never to act except on a maxim that can be willed as a universal law. Moral principles generally, e.g. 'Promises ought to be kept' are often said to be categorical imperatives, meaning that they are in no way conditional upon the wishes of those they apply to. (Cf. hypothetical imperative.)

COGNITIVISM. Any view according to which moral judgements are statements and therefore true or false.

COMPULSION. A person acts under compulsion when another person physically makes him act or, by a natural extension, gets him to act by severe threats. By a further extension *psychological* compulsions such as kleptomania (compulsive stealing) may also be recognised. Acts performed under compulsion are not performed freely, and their authors are accordingly not morally responsible (q.v.) for them.

CON-ATTITUDE. A term coined in order to refer generally to all 'anti' attitudes, e.g. of disapproval, dislike, aversion, etc.

CONCEPT. A person who understands the words 'good', 'free', 'triangle', etc. may be said to have the concepts of goodness, freedom, triangularity, etc. Whether a statement (locution) is analytic or synthetic, whether it follows from, is incompatible with, or independent of other statements, depends on the concepts involved. Philosophy, which is greatly concerned with the meanings of words and the logical relationships between statements, is often said to be CONCEPTUAL ENQUIRY as opposed, e.g. to factual enquiry or the exercise of moral judgement.

CONSCIENCE. Sometimes taken to be the name of the 'moral faculty'. Phrases involving the word can be interpreted on such lines as the following: 'to have a conscience' is to be sensitive to moral considerations, 'to have no conscience' is not to be sensitive to them, 'to consult one's conscience' is to exercise one's moral judgement.

CONSCIENTIOUSNESS. The disposition to act in accordance with one's moral judgements, to do what is thought to be right *because* it is thought to be right and from no ulterior motive.

CONTINGENT. Not necessary. *A posteriori* or empirical statements are contingent.

CULPABILITY. Liability for blame or punishment. To be culpable a person must, not only have done something held to be wrong, but also be responsible (q.v.) for what he did – he must not, e.g., have acted under compulsion (q.v.) or in ignorance (q.v.).

DESCRIPTIVE (or FACTUAL) MEANING. That aspect of the meaning of a word or phrase that has to do with reporting or describing as opposed to prescribing, evaluating, or expressing emotions or attitudes.

DETERMINISM. Any view according to which all actions are caused, predictable in principle, explicable according to scientific laws. Freewill problems are usually problems as to whether or not actions which are in some way determined can also be free in the sense relevant for moral responsibility.

DISAGREEMENT, IN ATTITUDE AND BELIEF. People disagree in belief when one asserts a statement and the other denies it. If what one asserts is true, the assertion of the other must be false. There can be disagreement in attitude between people who are not asserting any statements at all, as when one approves of something the other disapproves of. It is a question whether *moral* disagreement, e.g. about abortion or euthanasia, etc. is more a matter of disagreement in belief or in attitude.

DUTY (MORAL). Act held to be morally obligatory. For the perfect/imperfect duty distinction see chapter 2, pages 21–5; for the *prima facie*/strict duty distinction see chapter 2, pages 25–8; for the subjective/objective duty distinction see chapter 4, pages 44–6.

EGOISM (ETHICAL). The view that morality requires or at least permits one to set more store by one's own welfare than that of other people. (Cf. altruism, neutralism.) *Ethical* egoism is to be distinguished from *psychological* egoism, which is the view, not that people should or may, but that they, in fact, do prefer their own welfare to that of others.

EMOTIVE MEANING. That aspect of the meaning of a word or phrase that is a matter of expressing emotion or attitude rather than communicating factual information.

EMOTIVISM (THE EMOTIVE THEORY OF ETHICS). The view that moral judgements are exclusively or primarily linguistic vehicles for the expression of emotions or attitudes.

EMPIRICAL STATEMENT. A statement of which the truth or falsity can be established only by observation or experiment, a factual or *a posteriori* statement (q.v.).

'ETHICS'. Sometimes means the same as 'moral philosophy', other times refers to parts of the subject matter of moral philosophy. See note at end of chapter 1.

EVALUATIVE MEANING. Aspect of the meaning of a word or phrase which involves expressing a positive or negative assessment or rating. Consequently it is to be distinguished from descriptive or factual meaning. Prescriptivism and emotivism (q.v.) are differing accounts of evaluative meaning.

EXCULPATION, EXCUSE. Compulsion, for instance, exculpates in the sense that, if a person who has broken some rule can plead that he did so under complusion, he will not be held culpable for doing so. Factors which do not suffice to exculpate (remove guilt altogether) may excuse (reduce guilt) – e.g. health worries might be held to excuse neglect of responsibilities.

FACTUAL STATEMENT. Empirical or *a posteriori* statement, often as contrasted with moral or value judgement.

FREEDOM. It is a condition of moral responsibility that people act freely, i.e. not under complusion. It is a question whether actions which are caused (if actions can be caused) are free in the sense relevant to moral responsibility.

HYPOTHETICAL IMPERATIVE. An imperative in the form: 'If you want X, do Y' (Y being a means to X). Hence the opposite of a categorical imperative.

IDEAL. Area of morality distinguished from social morality as more personal and controversial.

IGNORANCE. A factor which, like compulsion, is held to exculpate in the sense that a person is not held responsible or culpable for what he does in ignorance.

INTUITIONISM. The view that certain moral judgements or principles can be 'seen' to be true, or that they are self-evident (q.v.). A species of ethical rationalism, usually involving the contention that there is some similarity in logical status between moral judgements and mathematical propositions.

'JUDGEMENT'. Term used in preference to 'statement' in the phrase 'moral judgement' and 'value judgement'. See note at end of chapter 5.

'LOCUTION'. Sometimes used in the text as a general word for referring to both factual *statements* and moral *judgements*. 'Statement' cannot be used as generally as in ordinary language because some moral philosophers deny that moral judgements are statements.

LOGIC. The systematic study of the rules of valid argument and all related matters. Logical points are contrasted with factual and moral ones. Thus it is a matter of logic that a square has four sides, a matter of fact that pillar boxes in Britain are red, and a matter of moral viewpoint that racial discrimination is morally bad.

MORAL PHILOSOPHY. The *philosophical* study of morality, to be distinguished therefore, from scientific or factual studies of morality (i.e. the psychology and sociology of morality) and from the expression of first order moral views.

'MORALISING'. Used in the text, without any derogatory intent, to refer to the expressing of first-order moral views.

NATURALISM (ETHICAL). Any view according to which moral judgements are factual (empirical) statements. 'Naturalism' is sometimes used more widely, as synonymous with 'cognitivism'. See chapter 5, pages 54 and 57–63.

NATURALISTIC FALLACY. The fallacy allegedly committed when moral words, 'good', 'right', 'ought', etc. are defined purely factually or descriptively, and when moral judgements are held to be deducible from factual statements.

NECESSARY CONDITION. Condition without which something cannot obtain or occur, contrasted with sufficient condition, i.e. condition given which something must obtain or occur. Thus having four sides is a necessary condition of being square, but not a sufficient one (a parallelogram has four sides but need not be square). Having three sides is, however, a sufficient condition of being a triangle.

NEUTRALISM (ETHICAL). The view that morality requires one to give exactly the same weight to one's own and anybody else's welfare. (Cf. altruism, egoism.)

NON-COGNITIVISM. Opposite of 'cognitivism'. Any view according to which moral judgements are not statements, but imperatives, expressions of attitude, etc.

OBJECTIVISM. Any view according to which moral judgements are statements about something other than the speaker's state of mind. Objectivist views are accordingly cognitivist, but some cognitivist views (e.g. the subjectivist view that moral judgements are about the speaker's attitudes) are not objectivist. Non-cognitivist views are normally felt by their opponents to be non-objectivist, but their supporters sometimes regard them as objectivist, especially when they stress the possibility of giving reasons for moral judgements. 'Objective' and 'subjective' spread much more darkness than light in moral philosophy.

PERSUASIVE DEFINITION. Definition which implies a value judgement, as when, e.g. 'freedom' is defined as 'conformity to law', with the conscious or unconscious hope that the favourable attitude commonly taken to freedom will be transferred to conformity to law.

POSITIVISM (MORAL). Any view which *identifies* morality with a current social code. See chapter 5, pages 52–3.

PRESCRIPTIVISM. The view that moral judgements have some important affinities with imperatives or commands. Prescriptivists hold that many expressions that are not imperative in form have PRESCRIPTIVE MEANING, and that the prescriptive meaning of terms like 'good' and 'ought' is primary, the descriptive secondary.

PRO-ATTITUDE. Opposite of a con-attitude (q.v.), e.g. approval, liking, desiring, etc.

PRUDENCE. Regard for one's own welfare.

RATIONALISM (ETHICAL). Views which construe moral judgements on the model of mathematical propositions. Certain moral judgements are held to be self-evident (q.v.). (Cf. intuitionism.)

RELATIVISM. Opposite of absolutism (q.v.).

RESPONSIBILITY. People are normally held morally responsible unless they act under compulsion or in ignorance. Moral responsibility is 'SUBJECTIVE' in the sense that 'mental factors' – the agent's knowledge and intentions – are taken into account when assessing his responsibility. To take an 'OBJECTIVE' view of responsibility would be to hold people responsible regardless of their state of mind.

SELF-EVIDENT. Traditionally, certain supposedly non-analytic statements, e.g. the axioms of geometry, have been held to be, so to say, *visibly* true. Intuitionists hold that this is also the case with certain moral judgements or principles. Developments in the philosophy of mathematics have rendered the notion of self-evidence obsolete.

'SOCRATIC PARADOX'. The view that nobody does what he is sincerely convinced he ought not.

SUBJECTIVISM. Opposite of 'objectivism' (q.v.).

SUFFICIENT CONDITION. See 'necessary condition'.

SUPEREROGATION. Act 'going beyond' duty.

SYNTHETIC. Opposite of 'analytic'. Factual, empirical, contingent, *a posteriori* statements are all synthetic. It is a matter of controversy whether any synthetic statements are *a priori* and necessary.

UNIVERSALISABILITY. The feature of moral judgements in virtue of which anyone who holds, e.g., that he ought to do such and such is committed to holding that everybody similarly circumstanced ought to act in a similar way. See chapter 6, pages 89–91.

UTILITARIANISM. The view that the whole of morality is, or should be, based on the PRINCIPLE OF UTILITY, namely, that one should aim at the greatest happiness of the greatest number.

VALUE JUDGEMENT. Moral judgements appear to be a species of value judgement. Aesthetic judgements are another. Many of the characteristics of moral judgements appear to be shared by value judgements generally. Accordingly the moral/factual, moral/logical contrasts appear to be special cases of a more general contrast between *value*, fact and logic.

VERIFICATION PRINCIPLE. The Logical Positivist principle that a synthetic statement is significant (meaningful) only if it is empirically verifiable.

VIRTUE. Quality of mind or character held to be admirable from the moral point of view.

Index